5/98

Ethnic Violence

Look for these and other books in the Lucent Overview Series:

Abortion	Illegal Immigration
Acid Rain	Illiteracy
Adoption	Immigration
Advertising	Memory
Alcoholism	Mental Illness
Animal Rights	Money
Artificial Organs	Ocean Pollution
The Beginning of Writing	Oil Spills
The Brain	The Olympic Games
Cancer	Organ Transplants
Censorship	Ozone
Child Abuse	The Palestinian-Israeli Accord
Cities	Pesticides
The Collapse of the Soviet Union	Police Brutality
Dealing with Death	Population
Death Penalty	Poverty
Democracy	Prisons
Drug Abuse	Rainforests
Drugs and Sports	The Rebuilding of Bosnia
Drug Trafficking	Recycling
Eating Disorders	The Reunification of Germany
Elections	Schools
Endangered Species	Smoking
The End of Apartheid in South Africa	Space Exploration
Energy Alternatives	Special Effects in the Movies
Espionage	Sports in America
Ethnic Violence	Suicide
Euthanasia	Teen Alcoholism
Extraterrestrial Life	Teen Pregnancy
Family Violence	Teen Sexuality
Gangs	Teen Suicide
Garbage	The UFO Challenge
Gay Rights	The United Nations
Genetic Engineering	The U.S. Congress
The Greenhouse Effect	The U.S. Presidency
Gun Control	Vanishing Wetlands
Hate Groups	Vietnam
Hazardous Waste	World Hunger
The Holocaust	Zoos
Homeless Children	

Ethnic Violence

by Mary Hull

WORLD IN CONFLICT

LUCENT *Overview Series*

Library of Congress Cataloging-in-Publication Data

Hull, Mary
    Ethnic violence / by Mary Hull.
        p.   cm. — (Lucent overview series)
    Includes bibliographical references and index.
    ISBN 1-56006-184-7 (alk. paper)
    1. Ethnic relations—Political aspects—Juvenile literature.
2. Political violence—Juvenile literature.   3. Culture conflict—
Juvenile literature.   I. Title.   II. Series.
    GN496.H85   1997
    305.8—dc21   96-40128
                                                                              CIP
                                                                               AC

Copyright © 1997 by Lucent Books, Inc.
P.O. Box 289011, San Diego, CA 92198-9011
Printed in the U.S.A.

Contents

Introduction

"THE EXPLOSION OF communal violence is the paramount issue facing the human rights movement today. And containing the abuses committed in the name of ethnic or religious groups will be our foremost challenge for years to come." This is the blunt assessment of the acting executive director of Human Rights Watch, a global monitoring group based in New York. There are currently between seven thousand and eight thousand linguistic, ethnic, or religious minorities in the world's 191 nations, fewer than 10 percent of which are ethnically or racially homogeneous. Only half of the countries with populations of over one million have a single ethnic group accounting for more than three-quarters of the population. Multiethnic states in Europe, Asia, Africa, and the Americas face the challenges of cooperation and conflict resolution. Amidst these attempts to unify, however, a growing number of politicians have tried to exploit ethnic differences to build followings for themselves.

Fueling ethnic tensions

Ethnic identity is one of the most firmly established features of societies everywhere. Around the planet, from Europe to Africa to Asia, ethnic identity is also at the root of violent conflict and civil war. In Rwanda, Bosnia, and elsewhere, members of opposing groups have committed atrocities—repeated acts of murder, rape, and torture—in the name of ethnic affiliation.

Overcrowding, poverty, and competition for economic resources have always fueled ethnic tensions, but today

these persistent problems are compounded by people's fears that they, as individuals and as nations, are losing their ethnic identification. As the world comes together commercially and culturally, its differences—religious, racial, linguistic, and historical—also collide. In this era of global interdependence, governments may fear a loss of sovereignty and people may fear a loss of heritage. Cooperation may mean sacrifice, and many compromises are seen as losses.

In Germany, neo-Nazi youth protest the immigration of non-Germans into their country. Attempts to maintain a national or ethnic identity often lead to violent conflicts.

As distinguished political scientist and historian Samuel Huntington has written, "The interactions among peoples of different civilizations enhance the civilization-consciousness of people that, in turn, invigorates differences and animosities stretching or thought to stretch back deep into history." While some ethnic conflicts are the contemporary manifestations of ancient problems that have never been solved, other ethnic conflicts are the result of political manipulation.

In an attempt to maintain national or ethnic identity, some groups retreat into rigid separatism, barricading themselves from outsiders or seceding from larger social groups with which they do not feel a kinship. Even when such actions are undertaken with the best intentions, to preserve a way of life, they generally lead to conflict.

Recognizing that ethnic tension can erupt wherever various cultures are mixed, global organizations such as the United Nations concentrate their efforts on preventing potential conflicts or resolving hostile disputes. The angry cycle of injustice, revenge, and retaliation associated with ethnic conflicts is not easily broken, however, particularly as ethnic rivalries more often exist within regions than between them. As the forces of modernization continue to bring different groups together, it has become more important than ever to acknowledge and understand ethnic differences. The ultimate solution to ethnic turmoil lies in identifying the roots of conflict and working to address tensions before they can reach the crisis stage.

1

The Roots of Ethnic Violence: How Conflicts Are Created

THE TERM *ETHNIC* is derived from the Greek word *ethnos*, meaning people. Today, ethnicity has a variety of definitions, but it commonly refers to the physical, social, or cultural distinctions a group of people share because of their ancestry and place of birth. Ethnic qualities can include physical appearance, language, religious beliefs, or social customs, in any combination. Ethnicity is an elastic term that can be stretched to identify a broad nationality, such as French, or shrunk to differentiate between the people of narrowly defined subgroups in France, such as Basques, Bretons, and Alsatians. Ethnicity distinguishes people of varying heritage who make up a national population. Though they are all citizens of one nation, for example, African Americans, Anglo-Americans, and Sioux Indians are ethnically distinct.

Ethnic identity

Though ethnic identification is part of how people view themselves, it is also a tool of classification used to define outsiders. In their native countries, inhabitants may identify themselves with a specific region or town, but as immigrants to a foreign land, they may be categorized simply by their national heritage. For example, in the United States, whether an immigrant hails from County

Cork or County Limerick, that person is simply "Irish" to American eyes. Similarly, a citizen of Britain might be called "European" in America; in Africa, the same person may be categorized even more broadly as "white."

Regardless of what country or region they come from, immigrants from the same country typically flock together. Sharing an ethnic identity within a community or a nation can provide feelings of kinship and familiarity. People of the same ethnic background may have much in common, from the love of certain foods and music to shared traditions and religious beliefs. In times of rapid change, ethnic ties provide a basis for trust. In lands where ethnic groups live within close proximity of each other, this trust typically implies an assurance that common interests are being protected.

Exploitation of ethnicity

Many leaders use an ethnic population's concern for protected interests as a platform to achieve political ends. Conflicts such as religious persecution or territorial dis-

An immigrant proudly stands in front of his Chinatown business. In this pocket of San Francisco, Asian immigrants have created a community with its own ethnic identity.

putes are often based on attempts by one ethnic group to maintain its interests and its way of life. Even if ethnicity is secondary to the conflict, connecting ethnicity with political or religious issues is a means of inspiring people to fight for a cause. In this way, ethnicity can become inextricably tangled with history, politics, religion, economics, or human rights issues. As ethnicity scholar Harold Isaacs has written, "History goes on being molded and remolded by each generation's needs, forever being enlisted and re-enlisted to serve new legitimizing, self-reinforcing, self-enhancing, self-rationalizing functions required by newly shaped political interests." Power seekers may use ethnic identification and a history of past oppression or glory to draw supporters who are willing to fight for political gain or territorial expansion—actions that in themselves they might otherwise feel are unjustified.

Ethnic divisions provide a convenient separating point for politicians who wish to divide a population into "us" and "them." Although ethnic violence can stem from ancient, unresolved conflicts, it is more often the result of attempts by individuals or factions to achieve political goals at the expense of a target populace. In periods of instability, charismatic leaders can exert tremendous power by exploiting the insecurities of an ethnic group.

The fragmentation of Yugoslavia

The war in Bosnia was caused in part by the exploitation of ethnic differences between Serbs and Bosnian Muslims. In 1991, Yugoslavia, which had been one of the largest multiethnic Communist nations, began to fragment: The republics of Croatia and Slovenia declared their independence first, followed the next year by Bosnia-Herzegovina. Later in 1992, Serbia and tiny Montenegro joined to form a separate country, the Federal Republic of Yugoslavia. In 1991 Muslims composed the largest single religious group in Bosnia-Herzegovina, but the new country was also home to two Christian populations: ethnic Serbs, who made up one-third of Bosnia's prewar inhabitants, and ethnic Croats.

The Serbs were led by men who believed that Bosnia had no right to exist as a state. The Serb leader, Radovan Karadzic, noting that the Roman emperor Caligula once appointed his horse as a senator, remarked, "That horse was more of a senator than Bosnia is a state." Karadzic argued that Bosnia belonged under Serb control because today's Bosnian Muslims are the descendants of Serbs who converted to Islam in 1389, after the Serbian state was conquered by Muslim forces of the Ottoman Empire. Serbs who refused to adopt the victors' religion were severely persecuted, and many were killed.

In the 1990s, however, Bosnians whose families had been Muslims for five centuries had no desire to change their religion, and most expected to live in peace with their Serb and Croat neighbors, some of whom likewise believed in the idea of a multiethnic Bosnian state. But Karadzic and other Serb leaders were able to use their version of history to fan the flames of ethnic rivalries that would lead to their political goal: the incorporation of Bosnian territory into the new Serb-dominated Yugoslavia.

A campaign of genocide

To ensure that the Serb state would be "ethnically pure" (populated by Serbs only), the Serbs began a campaign of genocide, the systematic elimination of an identifiable group of people. To remove Bosnian Muslims from the desired territory, Karadzic's followers uprooted more than 700,000 Muslims from their homes. The Serbs slaughtered tens of thousands of Muslim civilians and incarcerated others in concentration camps. Serb leaders even encouraged their soldiers to rape Muslim women, who would then give birth to Serbian babies and thus help "purify" the region. Predictably enough, however, the Bosnian Muslims fought back with a vengeance, and the conflict escalated.

Karadzic attempted to rationalize the atrocities by insisting that in liquidating the descendants of those who had cast their lot with Serbia's fourteenth-century enemies, his country was fighting Europe's "last anti-colonial war." Despite the centuries that have elapsed since the region's original resettlement by Muslims, Karadzic's comment draws on the belief that land previously occupied by one ethnic group rightfully belongs to that group even if that area is conquered and colonized by a foreign population. Colonialism, or the subjugation of a people and the acquisition of their land in the name of expanding the influence and territory of an empire, is an outdated practice, but lingering memories of stolen lands and displaced populations are at the heart of many ethnic conflicts that persist today.

The end of colonialism and the collapse of empires

In the eighteenth and nineteenth centuries many European nations raced to establish colonies in other continents. Colonialism created multiethnic states by importing

Ethnic conflict in Bosnia resulted in a devastating war. Innocent citizens were slaughtered by the thousands while others were displaced from their homes and forced to live in makeshift shelters (pictured).

and exporting settlers around the world. Great Britain sent its people to North America, Africa, and Asia. The Portuguese and the Spanish went to Latin America and Africa. The French established colonies in every part of the globe. Seeking resources, markets, and more land, these Europeans appropriated new territories and subjugated the native inhabitants under the new laws of the conquering state. Native religious practices and rules of order were often banned so the colonizing nation could impose and maintain its beliefs throughout its empire. Over time, civil unrest and the cost of maintaining colonies took its toll on distant parent governments. Though their influence remained strong in the subjugated cultures, the European powers failed to entirely suppress native ethnic practices and beliefs. Colonies became a financial burden, and many conquering states—especially those chiefly interested in resources or trade routes—loosened control and tried to maintain only an administrative presence in the colonies, a presence backed by military strength.

Twentieth-century changes

The twentieth century has been the story of the end of empires, and of the power struggles that have followed the breakdown of colonial control. When empires break down, controlling authority disappears, and the resulting instability encourages the flare-up of ethnic rivalries. Imperial rivalries led to World War I, which weakened the European empires and, together with successful anti-colonial movements, prompted their collapse.

World War I destroyed old systems of control and created new ones. In 1914, the Ottoman Empire had ruled much of eastern Europe, western Asia, and North Africa for five hundred years. The Hapsburg and Romanov empires ruled in central and parts of eastern Europe. Western empires—the British, the French, the Dutch, and the Belgian—ruled colonies in Asia and Africa. At war's end in 1918, the Western nations held on to some of their colonies (though their garrisons had been depleted by the demands for troops in Europe), but the Ottoman Empire had been

partitioned and the Hapsburg reign had ended. The Soviet Union (USSR) emerged, keeping intact the old Romanov empire as well as extending the imperial domains. In 1991, however, it too collapsed, defeated in part by economic woes and the desire for national self-determination among its territories.

In Moscow, Russians celebrate the collapse of the Soviet Union, which signaled the end of communism in Russia and the beginning of national self-determination.

The rise of ethnicity

When the Soviet Union disintegrated in 1991, many former satellite nations (countries controlled by the USSR) and former Soviet states (republics within the borders of the USSR) were left without central authority. The central Communist government was failing, and several of the former states and satellites saw the loosening of control as an opportunity to establish their own independence.

An elderly woman searches for relatives among corpses in war-torn Chechnya. Casualties continue to mount as Chechens fight for their independence from Russia.

The Soviet Union had always been a conglomeration of ethnic affiliations, but the fall of its empire allowed many territories previously identified as Soviet to construct nationalities around ethnic heritage, as in the former Soviet-controlled Yugoslavia. Even smaller ethnic divisions within former Soviet states have seized the opportunity to establish autonomy. Within Russia, for example, the republic of Chechnya is currently fighting for independence because the Chechens are ethnically distinct from the Russians who determine policy for all the Russian republics. "The collapse of the Soviet Union and Yugoslavia," writes professor Victor Zaslavsky, "[testifies] to the universality of nationalist sentiments and impulses toward separatism in all multiethnic Soviet-type societies."

Upon the breakup of the Communist power structure in Europe and Soviet-controlled Asia, the USSR dissolved into a score of new states, each with its own ethnic majorities and minorities. Individuals in these new nations have adapted to life in the emerging societies by activating kinship and ethnic ties. Resources, for example, that were once controlled by Soviet authority are now held by ethnic groups and distributed according to their interests and concerns. This poses a problem for minority ethnic groups in regions such as the Central Asian republics of the former Soviet Union, where scarce resources are allocated by majority groups. Writes Victor Zaslavsky:

> In Central Asia a considerable decline in per capita income, rapid deterioration of the ecological situation, and growing unemployment [have been] followed by intense interethnic conflict. In most instances, conflict arises over the distribution of resources and privileges within a given republic and competition is structured along ethnic lines.

In the absence of a unified Soviet order, many of these new self-governing territories face ethnic tensions that were once held in check by the presence of the Soviet military. Ethnic rivalries or the persecution of ethnic minorities are common, and these struggles threaten the stability of the newly independent states.

The fate of colonies

Since 1945, more than one hundred new states have come into the world, most of them former colonies that had never before existed as independent nations. Many of the subjugated people in these colonial states claimed a legitimate right to nationhood based on their previous habitation of colonized land. Natives of lands still subject to foreign control often use their prior occupation of a region to stir ethnic conflict. Northern Ireland, for example, is subject to British rule, and many of its residents consider themselves loyal British citizens. In this same region, though, Irish nationalists who favor unification of Northern Ireland and the Republic of Ireland (to the south) view the British as colonizers who appropriated the land and divided the Irish people against themselves.

Many times, issues of relinquishing lands to previous inhabitants are clouded by the history of human migration. Immigration creates conflicts because groups maintain lingering notions of priority based on earlier occupation. However, claims to prior ownership may be shaky if the inhabitants of a colonized territory were themselves conquerors who vanquished another indigenous people. For instance, the Matabele people of Zimbabwe feel they have a right to lands that were colonized by the Dutch three centuries ago. The Matabele, however, were not the original inhabitants of the land; they had acquired the land only by conquering and displacing tribes of San Bushmen already living in the area. Even peaceable migrant tribes are sometimes persecuted because they are not indigenous. Ceylon Tamils came to Sri Lanka from India as early as one thousand years ago, but their access to the land is limited because native Sri Lankans still consider the Tamils as immigrants.

One of the reasons immigrants, however old or new, are discriminated against, is because residents fear competition for jobs and economic opportunities. When a region experiences high unemployment and economic instability, anti-immigrant sentiment tends to increase.

Scapegoats and ethnic prejudice

Minorities and immigrants often are held responsible for declining economies, rising unemployment, and other national problems. When this happens, especially when the facts do not support the charges, the people who are singled out for blame are said to be scapegoats. Social segregation and a lack of communication between people of different ethnic backgrounds can reinforce the divisions that lead to blame and resentment. A group of people once scapegoated is vulnerable to discrimination by other groups—particularly majority groups—and treatment as inferior or second-class citizens. Regardless of whether the laws of the land proclaim equal justice for all citizens,

In Sri Lanka, ethnic violence has erupted between native Sri Lankans and Ceylon Tamils. Although the Tamils (pictured) immigrated to the country nearly one thousand years ago, they are still considered to be immigrants by native Sri Lankans.

the conduct of residents or public officials is not immune to beliefs that a different ethnic population is less deserving of rights. Living in a community with apparent ethnic divisions, even those who administer policy may consciously or unconsciously make legislative or judicial decisions based on ethnic distinctions rather than democratic principles.

Discrimination and antagonism

In 1995 police officers in Bradford, England, tried to arrest two Asian youths who were playing soccer in a neighborhood populated by Asians. The charge was "obstructing a path." The incident angered young people in the Bengali and Pakistani community, who already felt harassed by the police. Bengali and Pakistani Muslims in the Bradford area had long been suffering from racial discrimination in hiring, as well as an alarming Asian unemployment rate, which rose to 36 percent with the decline of textile employment in the area. Poor city schools with almost no Asian teachers also contributed to the hopelessness felt by Asian youths. Upset by the complacency of their elders, these young Muslims had formed a vigilante group to retaliate against perceived injustices from the police. A mob of three hundred Asian youths began hurling objects at police cars, firebombing stores, and torching parked cars. The riot lasted two days, and a force of three hundred officers had to be summoned from throughout England to reestablish order.

In the United States, claims of police brutality are often made against officers who apparently use excessive force more frequently against minorities. In 1992, police officers in Los Angeles County were prosecuted for police brutality against Rodney King, an African American who was beaten after being stopped for a traffic violation. Though the videotaped incident was replayed in the courtroom, a jury acquitted the officers of the charges. Within hours of the verdict, Los Angeles was the scene of large-scale violent rioting supposedly motivated by resentment against the unfair treatment of ethnic minorities in the

Children walk through the smoldering streets of Los Angeles following the Rodney King verdict. The city became the site of widespread rioting after white police officers were acquitted of beating an African-American man.

American justice system. The violence, however, occurred primarily between inner-city ethnic groups.

Interethnic rioting

South Central Los Angeles has witnessed ethnic tension and violence even between its ethnic minorities. During the outbreak of violence that followed the verdict in the Rodney King case, black and Hispanic rioters often singled out Korean-owned businesses as targets of looting. Along with anger at the system that acquitted the officers responsible for King's beating, the rioters were expressing their resentment toward Korean-Americans because of their economic success in the impoverished neighborhoods of the inner city. The rioters blamed the Koreans for the failure of blacks and Hispanics to establish an equal economic footing in their own community.

Such economically influenced ethnic prejudice is common in parts of the world where immigrant populations have prospered while indigenous people lack the financial strength to start businesses. Indians and Pakistanis in Africa, for example, are resented because they own the majority of businesses along that continent's eastern coast. In a similar position are the Chinese, who are prominent business owners in Southeast Asia, and the Tamils, who thrive economically in Sri Lanka. Ethnic groups whose members often play middleman roles between producers and consumers—such as retailers, peddlers, shopkeepers, and international traders—have been singled out for contempt by other groups throughout history. Though middlemen provide a valuable service to communities that have not developed their own network of local businesses, they are often envied and scorned by a population that wants to blame someone for its economic shortcomings. As a British economist notes:

> Taken as a whole, public opinion is hostile to the middleman. His function, and his hard work in bringing buyer and seller together, are ignored; profits are not regarded as a reward for labor, but as the result of sharp practices. Despite the fact that his very existence is proof to the contrary, the middleman is held to be redundant [unnecessary].

Modernization and ethnic conflict

When the benefits of modernity—whether social, educational, or economic—are not spread equally among ethnic groups, the uneven distribution typically leads to anger and distrust. As some ethnic groups in developing societies get a head start in the competition for the rewards of the modern world, tensions between groups are exacerbated. The disempowered or impoverished populations resent and envy the more successful, hence elite, ethnic groups because of their superior position in the new social hierarchy.

In the modern world of sudden population shifts, ethnic persecution, and oppression, it becomes difficult to identify all of the root causes of ethnic conflicts. The riots following the Rodney King verdict illustrate that violence can have multiple causes and that sometimes the

22

oppression of one ethnic group can prompt that group to release its aggressions against another ethnic group that is not responsible for the initial oppression. Through the videotaped beating and the media coverage of the ensuing riots, the Rodney King case also demonstrated that, whatever the cause of violence, ethnic conflicts will not go unnoticed by a modernized global community.

Advances in communications technology have shrunk the globe; time and distance have been conquered by the mobility of information. For millions of people, news of international issues and events can be accessed immediately. As one politician wrote in 1995, "We all live with one worldwide vocabulary: Chernobyl, Sarajevo, glasnost, ethnic cleansing, CNN." Ethnic conflicts are now televised. This growing interconnectedness has made it more difficult for states to behave in ways that outrage the world community. Technology has undermined the sovereignty of states. As a result of rapidly transmitted eyewitness accounts, there is now an increased concern for human rights violations around the globe.

Although modernization has worked to undermine the sources of conflicts, it has also contributed to ethnic tensions by increasing individual and group ambitions. Some of the fastest developing world economies have seen the worst ethnic violence in recent history. In Bombay, India, for example, ethnic conflict has kept pace with a rapidly growing economy as ethnic groups vie for superior economic positions. Because technology has significantly modified traditional modes of life, people fear a loss of identity. "The forces of modernization have given many people a sense that they don't belong anywhere, or that there's nothing permanent or stable in their lives," says Allen Kassof, director of the Project on

A man surveys the destruction of his business following the Los Angeles riots. Korean-owned businesses were often the targets of looting by blacks and Hispanics who resented the economic success of the Korean-Americans.

Ethnic Relations. "It's quite understandable that they then seek something that seems eternal and can't be taken away from them. One is membership in a group. Another is a belief system or religion."

Ethnic values and the resistance to change

The processes of economic modernization and social change around the world have separated many people from their traditional identities and ways of life. Religion—often in the form of movements that are labeled fundamentalist, indicating a strict adherence to a set of traditional or extreme principles—has provided a basis for identity in the face of this change. Many religions, including Islam, Judaism, Christianity, Hinduism, and Buddhism, contain fundamentalist factions. Some analysts see the rise of religious fundamentalism as a reaction against modernization and the dominance of Western culture (that is, the culture of progress that is spread by the industrialized world, which has touched the lives of many people in non-Western societies). While Western, especially American, culture, styles, and habits are popularized among many people abroad via film, television, and other mass media, a "de-Westernization" process is being embraced by some of the elites of non-Western societies, who had previously absorbed Western values and attitudes but now wish to return to regional values.

Traditional religious groups fear losing their heritage and becoming assimilated into the majority culture, and ethnic violence erupts out of this fear that modernization will render traditional practices obsolete and push aside ways of life believed to be sacred. In Egypt, differences between Islamic fundamentalists and the "Westernized" Egyptian government have resulted in a terrorist campaign in which the fundamentalists seek to overthrow the secular government and institute *sharia* (Islamic law). These Egyptian fundamentalists believe their government has sold out to the West and abandoned the principles of Islam. They see the Islamic religion as a force for rejecting Western culture. "Western colonialism has gone," explains

In Cairo, Egypt, a billboard condemns the use of terrorism by Islamic fundamentalists who wish to overthrow the "Westernized" government and institute Islamic law.

an Egyptian scholar of Islamic theology, "but we still have not completed our independence. We will not be free until Egypt becomes a Muslim state."

Adhering to religion and other traditional practices is one method that people use to resist the rapid changes inherent in the modern world. Living at a time when technological advances make even yesterday's truths seem outdated, many people cling to traditional beliefs for stability and meaning. Playwright, poet, and former Czech president Vaclav Havel reflected on this phenomenon by stating: "Our civilization has essentially globalized only the surface of our lives. But our inner self continues to have a life of its own. And the fewer answers the era of rational knowledge provides to basic questions of human being, the more deeply it would seem that people, behind its back as it were, cling to the ancient certainties of their tribe." Insecurity brought on by the transforming forces of modernization has emphasized group differences, leading in turn to fragmentation. The world has been globalized by science and technology and economic modernization, but at the same time, it has been fragmented into many different parts more fiercely assertive than before.

2

Nationalism and Ethnic Violence

ETHNICITY IS THE primary unit of social organization in some areas of the world. In parts of Asia and Africa, ethnicity is more important than other measures of difference, such as class and nationality. However, in much of the Western world, nationality, class, politics, and religion have emerged as the main societal divisions. These divisions, though based on the same underlying principle of group difference as ethnicity, are cross-cutting divisions. For example, Western political parties incorporate people of many different ethnicities; party affiliation has more to do with philosophical and economic allegiances than ethnic ones.

The forces of European history are responsible for this structuring of social divisions along national, religious, political, and class lines, rather than ethnic ones. In the 1500s, the Protestant Reformation split European Christians into Catholic and Protestant camps that did not correspond to, for example, linguistic differences. That is, both Catholics and Protestants continued to speak German, French, or English, according to their national origins. Similarly, the late-eighteenth-century Industrial Revolution created working classes of all ethnic backgrounds whose members formed like-minded political parties. People of the same ethnic group were also distributed among the different classes. This is in marked contrast to much of Africa, for example, where ethnic groups tend to be either prosperous as a group or poor as a group. As a result of cross-cutting forces in Western history, people were offered alternative identities, and they tended to identify themselves by class or national background rather than by ethnic group.

The concept of ethnicity is the extension of family to the largest social level, until it becomes one big community with a common ancestor. Similarly, a nation, though not a family, is viewed as a large community with a common history and way of life. Professor Benedict Anderson has described a nation as an "imagined community"—imagined because "members of even the smallest nation will never know most of their fellow-members, meet them, or even hear of them, yet in the minds of each lives the image of their communion." Broader in scope than kinship or ethnic affiliations, the nation is the largest unit that commands group loyalty. In many parts of the world, nationality has taken the place of ethnicity as the primary means of personal identification. Nationalism, a kind of patriotism or fraternity on a grand scale, has inspired millions of people to risk their lives for the sake of national pride.

Defining nationalism

Nationalism is a term that historians apply quite broadly to describe the feeling that members of a nationality may share as a result of certain common cultural characteristics, including language, customs, manners, and literature. Members of a nationality may also believe that they share a common history. They may share a love for their fellow nationals, not necessarily as individuals, but as people who share similar basic beliefs. Sociologist and historian Eugene Lemberg defines nationalism as a "system of ideas, values, and norms, an image of the world and society [which makes a] large social group aware of where it belongs and invests this sense of belonging with a particular value. In other words, it integrates the group and demarcates its environment." Outsiders to the nation therefore become "foreigners."

People of the same nationality often share similar values, cultural characteristics, and a common history. These aspects help form a sense of nationalism and create a common civic identity. This Serbian man wears pins and carries signs to show his nationalism during a rally.

All immigrants are at one time "foreign," so inclusion in a country that is creating a national identity may be problematic. By attempting to integrate diverse faiths and cultures into a common civic identity, nationalist movements face the difficulty of having to suppress some of the extremely "foreign" characteristics of the citizenry in order to foster a feeling of unity that is moderately tolerable to all. In doing so, nationalism has both subdued ethnic conflicts and provoked them.

As a political force, nationalism has shaped the history of Europe and the world over the last two centuries. Achieving national unity and independence became a kind of religion in nineteenth-century Europe, when France, Italy, Germany, Spain, and England all experienced unifying nationalist movements. Nationalism has led to expansionism and the creation of empires, but nationalism has also encouraged states to become self-determined and to escape from oppressive empires. The collapse of the USSR, for example, paved the way for the emergence of independent nation-states, but liberation did not come without crisis and violent conflict. Thus nationalism has the capacity to be both a destructive and a liberating force. This is illustrated by some of the forms nationalism has taken in the modern world. Nationalism may be promoted by established nations that seek to project a sense of who they are and protect what they see as the fundamental nature of their society from change. Nationalism also arises in emerging nations that wish to establish a separate identity or fight outside control. In addition, those who seek to transform an existing state into an ethnically "pure" or homogeneous entity may use an ethnically exclusive form of nationalism, or ethno-nationalism, to further their cause.

Nationalism and ethnic pluralism

Because it is based on self-determination, nationalism is allied with liberalism, the belief in the freedom of the individual. While nationalism seeks to forge a common civic identity among a population, the very existence of this sense of national consciousness hinges on the freedom of these people to choose their own identity. Alexis de Tocqueville, a young French visitor to the United States over 150 years ago, was describing this phenomenon when he wrote that free and liberal societies were likely to nourish a diversity that could undermine the very social cohesion on which their stability depended.

Throughout U.S. history, dominant social groups have feared the influx of immigrants, especially those from places other than northern Europe, believing that they were bringing with them ideas and practices that threatened the fundamental character of American society. Despite the capacity for the United States to absorb wave after wave of immigrants, this debate continues today in questions such as whether bilingualizing the United States will change the nature of American society or whether an emphasis on multiculturalism is eroding a common civic and national identity.

Today many Europeans also fear that heavy overseas immigration is changing the character of their nations. After World War II, a boom in the Western European economy caused a labor shortage which attracted millions of foreign workers, many of them from North Africa, Turkey, and the West Indies. These immigrants migrated primarily to cities in France, Germany, and Britain. In the

1970s, when unemployment increased in Europe, many Western European governments took measures to halt the immigration of foreign workers, and to encourage immigrants to leave. Most immigrants did not wish to return to their places of origin, especially since the second and third generations felt little attachment to their parents' and grandparents' native lands. The current xenophobia in Western Europe reflects an economic crisis that has increased unemployment rates and heightened competition for limited resources. Economic troubles exacerbate national tensions. Although many nonmaterial factors such as culture and tradition affect people's attitudes toward immigration, as scholar John Steinbrunner of the Brookings Institution contends, "There isn't a nationality problem anywhere in the world that cannot be solved by economic prosperity."

Immigration and ethnic violence

The mass importation of people into an area can lead to ethnic conflict because previous inhabitants may feel that their way of life will be jeopardized by the mixing of cultures. To maintain control over their ethnic identity, some nations may oppress immigrant groups and categorize

North African immigrants await inspection by French immigration officers in this 1974 photograph. When Europe's unemployment rate rose during the 1970s, immigration of foreign workers was halted to ensure that jobs would not be taken from native Europeans.

them as inferior people who have less right to live in the host country. In the age of colonialism, Africans were brought to America as slaves, and after the Industrial Revolution, Asians migrated to America and to Africa to build railroads. Today, these groups are reclaiming their ethnic heritage, and in some cases this has sparked controversy and even violence, because racially motivated hatred has existed in American society since the time when these groups were considered inferior to people of European descent. More recent concerns over the migration of Hispanic peoples from Central America and Mexico has continued to challenge the notion of the United States as a tolerant, immigrant nation.

In a similar manner, the migration of former colonial subjects to the countries that controlled them has also generated ethnic tension. Indians, Pakistanis, Africans, and West Indians have historically migrated to Great Britain to seek education and job opportunities. Indonesians and Eurasians have gone to the Netherlands. Algerians and Vietnamese have immigrated to France in large numbers. Fearing that the large-scale arrival of people from different ethnic groups was changing the character of their societies, several European countries have tightened their immigration and naturalization policies.

Protesters display signs with anti-immigration messages during a rally organized by the group "America for Americans."

German nationalism

In Germany, where nationality laws make citizenship dependent on German bloodlines rather than birthplace, someone from another ethnic group can gain citizenship only after passing elaborate tests of German language, history, and culture. The process, which typically takes ten to fifteen years, can be hard on migrant populations. For example, only about 1 percent of Germany's two million residents who are ethnic Turks have full citizenship rights, including the right to vote. Ethnic Turks, who are the children and grandchildren of Turks who migrated in search of jobs after World War II, have been the victims of ethnic violence in Germany. "The [citizenship] law effectively brands all foreigners in Germany as not belonging there and so encourages ethnic violence," says *Foreign Policy* editor Charles William Maynes. Defining this population as not-German has made it easier for people of German heritage to blame the Turks for a host of national problems, from the loss of employment opportunities to the corruption of German ethnicity. In 1993 the deliberate torching of a Turkish home in Solingen, Germany, claimed the lives of two Turkish women and three Turkish girls. Turks fought back by demonstrating in cities throughout Germany. They demanded full recognition as German citizens and protection from violence aimed at their communities. So far Germany's reaction has been to toughen its immigration laws.

Ethnic tensions in countries like Germany that have strict immigration and naturalization laws have prompted violence and sometimes riots by groups who are residents of the land but have not been granted the rights and privileges of the ruling ethnic party. Very few of the world's 191 countries, with the exception of Japan and Germany,

Five ethnic Turks were killed when German arsonists set fire to this home in Solingen, Germany. Hundreds of Turks gathered at the site to offer prayers for the victims and to voice their discontent over the status of Turks in Germany.

are primarily ethnically homogeneous. However, some multiethnic states have been more successful than others at creating an inclusive national identity.

The changing identity of nations

France contains a mixture of ethnic groups, including German-speaking Alsatians, Italian-speaking Corsicans and residents of the eastern Riviera, Catalans and Basques among the Pyrenees, Celtic Bretons, and Flemings in northern provinces near Belgium. Today it also contains a large overseas population, including many immigrants from France's former colonial holdings in North Africa and Asia.

France has had difficulty coming to terms with the heavy migration of non-French peoples, particularly from North Africa. France is a multicultural nation in the sense that it has always incorporated immigrants, but newcomers have been assimilated into prevailing French culture. In this way, multicultural France has retained one national identity. Now the French fear that the Muslim arrivals, particularly the extreme fundamentalists, will be unassimilable. If they are not willing to accept a level of "Frenchness," the immigrants may pose a threat to the current state of French nationhood, but if they are assimilated, the French identity may be transformed. In 1988, fears about Muslim distinctiveness drove a national debate when three young Muslim girls insisted on wearing veils over their heads at school. Assimilationists, those who seek to transform new immigrants into French citizens, thought their demand was intolerable because it threatened one of the functions of the school system, which has been to homogenize immigrants into French culture. Recent incidents of Algerian terrorism in France, combined with high unemployment, have added to anti-immigrant sentiment, causing France to aim for a "zero immigration" policy.

Political parties of the extreme right in Europe, such as Jean-Marie Le Pen's National Front in France and the former West German Republican Party, have used complaints about "foreign invasion" to further their political goals. Negative response to the stream of arrivals from overseas has led France to tighten its borders and enact measures to expel illegal immigrants. The French interior minister spoke on the issue in 1993, stating, "France has been a country of immigration, and no longer wants to be." The influx of newcomers has challenged the national concept of "Frenchness" and sparked a debate as to whether the culture can absorb the tide of immigrants. Some nations are more willing to incorporate different ethnic groups into their societies than others. Nationalism, where it seeks to incorporate people based on a common civic identity, can serve this purpose. However, when nationalism is identified with only one ethnic group or ruling party, it is known as ethnically exclusive, or ethno-nationalism. In severe cases, ethno-nationalist movements can lead to violence and even genocide, in the attempt to make a state ethnically "pure" or homogeneous.

Ethno-nationalist movements

"Nation," writes political philosopher Ghia Nodia, is another name for "We the People." However, the process of determining who belongs to "We the People" can be a bloody one, leading to civil war or genocide. Nationalism, like patriotism, inspires citizens to defend and protect the nation they cherish by rallying people to a common cause, even if that cause is based on the oppression of specific ethnic groups. As a result, misguided or corrupt nationalist sentiments can become ethno-nationalist movements and help to arouse disrespect, racism, xenophobia, and anti-Semitism. "Nationalism," writes former British foreign secretary Geoffrey Howe, "can all too easily pervert love and pride for one's country into hatred and contempt for others, into the desire to dominate and displace." Ethno-nationalism can be internal, directed at the country in which it evolves, or it can be external, directed outwards at other areas of the world.

In the late 1930s, ethno-nationalism motivated Germany's Adolf Hitler to annex territory in Austria and Czechoslovakia that was populated by ethnic Germans. Drawing on a century-old concept of *volkgeist*—a nationalist spirit based

During the late 1930s, ethno-nationalism motivated Nazi Germans to embark on a genocidal campaign; German citizens who were considered undesirable or of "impure" origins were enslaved or massacred by the Nazis.

on folk traditions, kinship, and assumed heroic virtue—Hitler's National Socialist (Nazi) Party pursued policies of genocide in the name of German ethno-nationalism. Part of Nazi doctrine was its assertion of racial supremacy. Hitler and his party wanted to make Germany an ethnically "pure" state by enslaving or killing off undesirable citizens or people of "impure" origins. As a result, many Jews, Slavs, Gypsies, and even the insane and mentally handicapped were either imprisoned or murdered in the name of "ethnic cleansing." Such assertions of racial supremacy, which can be fanned by ardent ethno-nationalism, are still found at the core of many ethnic conflicts today.

Ethnic identity and national organization

Citizenship in ethno-nationalist societies is not open to all who meet the immigration requirements, as in the United States. Ethno-nationalism usually demands that a person belong to a particular ethnic or religious group in order to enjoy the rights of citizenship, and those who cannot claim this ethnic or religious identity face discrimination. Turks in Germany, who have a difficult time becoming German citizens, are one example of a group that is disadvantaged by an exclusive nationalism.

Ethnic identity proved a useful tool for the political and national organization of the nations created since 1945, particularly former colonies, many of which were multi-ethnic societies that had no common identity, civic culture, institutions, or sense of national purpose around which to build a nation. Often nations that were once colonies were stuck with borders that were determined to serve the parent nation's interests in land and natural resources without regard for various ethnicities that were divided or hemmed in by boundary lines on a map.

Creating nations where they do not exist

Nationalism and the idea of a nation-state are not traditional notions in many cultures, particularly in much of the developing world. In many areas, identity has historically lain with ethnicity rather than nationality. Consequently, it can be difficult to impose national borders where none have previously existed.

In Africa, the sheer number and diversity of ethnic groups made it impossible for colonial governments to draw national borders that reflected every ethnic division.

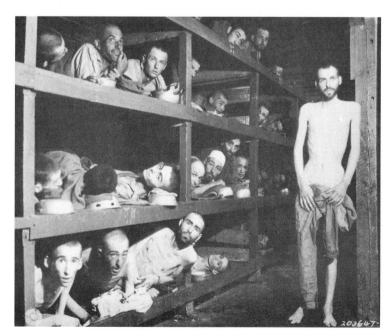

In an effort to "purify" Germany, Nazis mercilessly slaughtered or imprisoned all non-German citizens. Hordes of Jews, Slavs, and Gypsies were forced to endure horrendous treatment in concentration camps throughout Germany.

Colonial powers created territories out of clusters of loosely linked villages, and although borders were at times redrawn in response to ethnic demands, inevitably some groups were thrown together while others were divided. Rwanda, formerly a Belgian colony, is an example of a country whose borders were drawn by colonialists to encompass two adjacent yet historically antagonistic ethnic groups, the Hutu and the Tutsi. These two ethnic groups have engaged in a power struggle that has resulted in periodic outbursts of ethnic violence since the breakdown of colonial control in the early 1960s. Subordinating ethnic loyalties to national allegiance has been a challenge for Rwandans. Being Rwandan means less than being Hutu or Tutsi or Belgian, for example. A Hutu citizen of Rwanda is apt to have more in common with a Hutu from Burundi than with a Rwandan from a different ethnic affiliation.

Edmund Keller, director of UCLA's African Studies Center, has written:

> Assuming that the most efficient manner in which to cast off the yoke of colonialism was to accept uncritically the notion of a multiethnic nation-state, African leaders universally embraced this idea. They set about the business of instilling in their followers the principle of "dying as tribes and being born as nations". . . but very few of these states possessed the needed cultural basis.

A Rwandan child searches for her parents among the dead. Rwanda has been torn apart by the ethnic conflict between the rival Hutu and Tutsi populations.

Despite efforts by these states to instill a national consciousness among their citizens, identity continues to lie with ethnicity.

Encompassing ethnicities: the former Yugoslavia

The former Yugoslavia is another example of a country whose borders bear little relation to the placement of different ethnic populations. Promoting the concept of nationalism within artificial borders is no easy task, but as the historian Ernest Gellner has written, "Nationalism is not the awakening of nations to self-consciousness; it invents nations where they do not exist." Nationalism may be an imagined community, but such a community is easier to create in areas where ethnic groupings are already homogeneous. Bosnia-Herzegovina has been struggling with its multiple ethnic groups and their desire to establish boundaries for themselves. Since people of various ethnicities are spread throughout the nation, attempts to create such borders would be problematic at best. Not surprisingly, problems of national identity and ethnic conflicts have been acute in the Balkans. It has not been possible to propose borders that satisfy all the groups involved, and consequently there has been much resistance to the concept of multiethnic nationhood.

In some cases, imperial powers purposely drew colonial borders so as to encompass antagonistic ethnic groups. Soviet policy, for example, ignored existing ethnic boundaries. In the words of professor Victor Zaslavsky, "In accordance with a [Soviet] divide-and-conquer policy, the borders between ethnic territories were often drawn arbitrarily, in obvious contradiction to historical traditions or existing ethnodemographic situations [population densities]." Many of the former Soviet republics contained two or more ethnic groups with historically poor relations, and often a single ethnic group would be divided among two or more republics. The Soviet borders were engineered to promote internal conflict, which would then impede ethnic groups from uniting to overthrow the Communist system.

This policy was also designed to force disputing groups to look to Moscow for protection from one another. Since gaining their independence, the post-Soviet states must deal with ethnically exclusive, even aggressive, nationalisms stemming from their being thrown together with antagonistic ethnic groups. Today, the ethnic groups seek to form their own nations. They want territory, political independence, and privilege, often at the expense of other peoples.

Separatist nationalism

Europe's retreat from world leadership after WWII was caused in part by the success of anticolonial movements among colonies in Asia and Africa that sought to eliminate imperial control. In most cases, freedom was won only after long bouts of guerrilla warfare convinced the colonial powers that the cost of maintaining colonies was too great. With the recent collapse of the USSR, the last of the great European empires, similar separatist movements have sprung up all over Russia.

Currently a separatist nationalist conflict rages in Chechnya, a former Soviet autonomous region that declared its independence from Russia in 1991. Chechnya lies along the Caucasus, the nine-hundred-mile mountain range between the Black and Caspian Seas that is home to fifty ethnic groups representing Turkish, Middle Eastern, Eastern European, and Caucasian civilizations. Among the Chechens, there is a strong tradition of nationalism and independence going back to Chechnya's resistance to the sixteenth-century Russian empire of Ivan the Terrible. Ethnic differences have contributed to disagreements between the Chechens and the rulers of Russia and the former USSR. Because the Chechens, unlike most other Caucasian peoples, have no hierarchically organized, or vertical, social structures, their ethnic group is organized horizontally into clans. This means that power is shared among the clans, with no overall ruler. When czarist Russia, the Soviet Union, and modern Russia tried to govern the Chechens, they found no central figure or Chechen leader they could install as regional authority. As a result, each would-be conqueror has had to bring in an outside governor to manage Chechnya. These governors have not only been resented as foreigners and conquerors, but the role they are supposed to fulfill makes no sense to the Chechens, who are not used to power coming from one individual. Chechens' ethnic distinctiveness, including their organization of power through clans, has fueled their struggle for independence and impeded attempts to conquer them. As a result of their unruliness, the Chechens were deported from their ancestral lands by Joseph Stalin in 1944 and forced to resettle in Siberia and Kazakhstan. The Chechens were later "rehabilitated," and those who have returned to their homeland are determined not to lose it to Russian force again.

The role of history

History plays a major role in promoting the Chechen desire for autonomy, as their past oppression has generated ethnic solidarity and fueled their sense of nationalism. The relationship between history and nationalism is also evident in the practice of vendetta, the desire and obligation to avenge past injustice, which plays a large role in ethnic conflict. During their war for independence, for example,

Chechens faithfully recorded the serial numbers on invading Russian fighter planes so that at some future date they could trace the pilot and kill him or his family. Knowledge of this practice motivated the Russians to kill even more Chechens, to protect themselves and their children.

One of Russian president Boris Yeltsin's advisers, acknowledging the relationship between history and conflict, says of resolving the situation in Chechnya, "the task is to make a man forget his memories." Yet the Chechens and other ethnic groups have strong memories of their oppression and manipulation at the hands of Soviet nationality policy, whose legacy is ethno-nationalist movements in many of the post-Soviet states. Condemning the bloodshed in such separatist conflicts, former Soviet academician Aleksandr Yakovlev urges, "The 21st century world must call into question the right of each people to its own statehood on the mere ground that this people is a national entity."

An increasingly democratic world offers more opportunities to express both national and ethnic aspirations and antipathies. The end of the cold war, for example, brought both a wave of democratization and a revival of nationalism in the former Communist states. Nationalism, when it is based on an inclusive civic identity, can help to create civic organizations and enthusiasm that provide the basis for participatory democracy. However, in ethnically divided societies, democratization can lead to the tyranny of a majority ethnic group over minorities. For the people who live in areas affected by ethnic strife, concepts of nationalism, ethnicity, and self-determination have had serious practical consequences in their everyday lives.

3

Living in a
Troubled Land

GENERATIONS MAY GROW UP without ever having known peace; living with conflict and even violence may become normal. In some places, violence is a fact of life. When people of various ethnic backgrounds live in the same region but share no nationalist spirit, the separate factions typically try to impose their own views of nationhood upon the land. The resulting clash is often violent, and depending on the strength and conviction of each faction, the violence may persist for a long time. In severe cases, ethnic conflicts force families to leave their homes and towns, and children find their lives suddenly disrupted and changed forever. Ethnically motivated violence can be brutal, and survivors face the task of putting lives back together again and functioning as families and citizens.

Northern Ireland: two cultures

In Northern Ireland, ethnic hatred has existed for many generations. The conflicts revolve around disagreements between citizens of differing cultural, economic, political, and religious backgrounds. Northern Ireland is a territory of Great Britain, though geographically it is a part of the island of Ireland. The Protestants of Northern Ireland are descendants of seventeenth-century colonizers from England and Scotland. They are the majority; they own most of the land and businesses, hold most of the power, and look to Great Britain to help them maintain their position.

The Catholics of Northern Ireland, however, are descended from the original inhabitants of the island of Ireland. Many of them desire independence from the United Kingdom. Inspired by the African-American movement for civil rights in the United States, Catholics in Northern Ireland began protesting inferior living conditions in the 1960s, particularly disparities in housing and employment. Studies of the composition of local government bodies called district councils in Northern Ireland showed that Catholics were significantly underrepresented, particularly at higher levels. This lack of representation was the result of council discrimination against Catholics. Today, research by the Fair Employment Commission (FEC) shows that many of the councils continue to discriminate against Catholics. This reinforces the belief that Unionists, those who want to remain British subjects, are not willing to share power in Northern Ireland.

When Catholics began protesting their living conditions in the 1960s, Protestants responded with counterdemonstrations against Catholics, and the bombings, shootings, and bloodshed known as "the Troubles" began. The con-

This 1971 photograph captures the belligerent atmosphere of Northern Ireland as masked children and teens militantly march through the streets. Religious and political affiliations have kept Northern Ireland segregated and on the verge of civil war.

British soldiers walk past the bombed-out remains of a building while patrolling the streets of Enniskillen, Northern Ireland.

flict pits Catholics against Protestants and loyalists against nationalists. Prejudiced views held by Catholics and Protestants alike fuel discrimination and dislike; these stereotypes are perpetuated by continued self-imposed segregation, which tends to intensify fierce loyalties to religious and political affiliations. Slight differences in accent and speech patterns are used to establish identity, and determine "which foot someone kicks with," the local term for whether someone is a Protestant or Catholic. According to one resident, "People have ways of finding out whether you're Catholic or Protestant by your accent, your address, where you went to school, and certain interests— for example, what football team one supports."

Signs of violence

Decades of terrorism have so traumatized Catholics and Protestants in Northern Ireland that everyday occurrences seem threatening and signs of violence seem ordinary. "Living there," says one resident, "you become suspicious, of parked cars, trucks parked outside your house, running people (you think why are they running?), packages, and bags left in shops. You see a bag left and you tell the police and they will cordon off that area, treat it like a bomb." On the other hand, residents take for granted police carrying guns (normally British police patrol unarmed) and civilians with weapons. Many families have members who belong to one of the paramilitary wings of the competing factions, so violence has become part of family life as well. In Northern Ireland, where unemployment is high and standards of living are low, joining the paramilitaries can mean "becoming somebody" for a young man.

Paramilitary action

Both the loyalists and nationalists have paramilitary organizations, the most prominent of which are known respectively as the Ulster Volunteer Forces (UVF) and the Irish Republican Army (IRA). In addition to working to undermine each other's cause, the paramilitaries police their own communities, sometimes ruthlessly. In Belfast, for example, a Catholic passenger in a car that rear-ended another automobile belonging to an IRA chief was punished for joyriding and for his disrespectful behavior. The twenty-year-old had his legs thrust through the pickets of a steel fence and battered with steel pipes. Punishment beatings like this are used by the paramilitary organizations to enforce discipline within their communities.

During an eighteen-month cease-fire, which ended in April 1996, the paramilitaries maintained a high profile within their communities. While the truce held high-profile acts of terrorism in check, more than one hundred punishment beatings were administered during the official cease-fire. "We are opposed to punishment beatings, and will not condone them," says Martin McGuiness, second-in-command of the IRA's political wing, Sinn Féin; however, vigilantism has a measure of popular support. Because many citizens do not trust the police, they look to the paramilitaries to prevent crime and to punish criminals. "There is no doubt that some people—not the majority—approve of the beatings," says Chief Inspector Peter Kane of the Royal Ulster Constabulary, the British police force in Northern Ireland. "In some areas, especially those plagued by joyriders or drug dealers, they are popular. But you can't call what they have handed out justice, by any means."

Crossing boundaries

Young people in the north, especially those who have lived in troubled areas, grow up nervous, unwilling to leave the relative safety of their neighborhoods. Youth workers try to organize cross-community activities for young people in Belfast, but though Catholic and Protestant teens mix while on a youth trip, once they return home they do not see each other because they do not socialize outside their own neighborhoods. In some areas it is unsafe for friends from the two groups to meet each other at home.

Cross-community work is being done by some churches, and women's groups, seniors groups, and ministries also try to bring Catholics and Protestants together. "Everyone can sit down together and have tea," says one resident, "but after something happens [a paramilitary or terrorist action] there is a real tension in the air. As a Catholic, you feel guilty when the IRA does something, even though you have nothing to do with it. You feel as if you have to apologize, you try to say 'we're not all like this in our community.'"

Community ties and kinship networks are strong sources of help in desperate times. For example, some provos, or fighters, in the IRA are constantly on the run and often cannot stay in one place for more than two nights in a row. They rely on those sympathetic to the nationalist cause to house or shelter them when necessary. Ethnic ties provide a basis for trust in situations of conflict. Kinship networks like those in Northern Ireland are activated in times of need, and families and strangers who share an ethnic bond cooperate to achieve a shared goal.

Family separation in the Bosnian war

In war-torn Bosnia, families were often separated as part of the Serb plan to weaken the Muslim resistance movement and prevent the Bosnian Muslims from reproducing. Men were rounded up and killed or sent to concentration camps where they were starved and tortured. Women were also killed or taken to camps where many of them were made sexual prisoners. By starving, torturing, killing, and raping mostly Bosnian Muslim civilians, the Serbs were carrying out a policy of "ethnic cleansing," meant to destroy the Bosnian Muslims and drive their survivors out of conquered territory.

Azra, a Bosnian Muslim woman, was fifteen when she gave this account of the Serb evacuation of her town:

> They separated the men from the women and children. There are no words to describe it. They took my father away. He cried as we were saying goodbye; I had never seen him cry before. Some of the men stayed with us; the rest were taken to prison camps at Omarska and Keraterm. My father was in that group; I believe he is now dead. The rest of my family was my mother, my sister, ten, and my mentally retarded brother, 18. They transported us to a prison camp at Trnopolje.

Azra and thousands of other Bosnian Muslim women, as well as some Croatian women, were repeatedly raped by Serb soldiers while detained in prison camps. In an effort to "purify" the next generation of Bosnians, the women were deliberately impregnated, held captive, and released only after a pregnancy was too advanced to abort.

Women who have been raped in Bosnia face difficult futures. Many of the victims fear they will not be accepted back into their communities. Some fear rejection from

A Muslim woman cries over the grave of her husband, who was killed during the siege of Sarajevo. During the war in Bosnia, Serbs routinely raped, tortured, and killed Muslim civilians as part of their "ethnic cleansing" of Serbian territory.

©1994 Worldwide Copyright by CARTOONEWS INTERNATIONAL Syndicate N.Y.C., USA

"Now that you've learned your lesson, fellow Bosnians, I'm ready to discuss peace."

their husbands. Others want to kill the children created by this violence, or even kill themselves. Many of the victims experience self-hatred as a result of the trauma. All of these feelings serve to prevent women from speaking about the violence directed at them or from admitting that they were raped or enslaved.

Enslavement in Serbian camps

Mirsada was seventeen in 1992 when she escaped from a Serb camp where she and a thousand other women had been sexually enslaved, raped nightly by soldiers and forced to cook for and serve them. She recalled the day the Serb soldiers rounded up the people of her village. "They dragged my neighbor, a Serb, and his entire family out of the house. As he was not a member of the Serbian militia and had refused to kill Muslims and Croats, they took his 12-year-old sister Zeljka to the camp." Later

Zeljka's brother Rade came to the camp and helped Zeljka, Mirsada, and a dozen others to escape. They hid in improvised underground shelters. Two of them were caught, but the others managed to get away.

"If it hadn't been for Zeljka's brother, I would not have survived," Mirsada told the workers at the refugee camp where she later took shelter. "I spent over four months in that camp. . . . Most of the girls did not survive. They murdered many girls, slaughtered them like cattle. . . . It is a nightmare that cannot be described or understood. . . . I want to forget everything. I cannot live with these memories."

Memory

The systematic use of rape as an instrument of war to practice ethnocide (the destruction of an ethnicity) against the Bosnian Muslim culture and people has demoralized Bosnian Muslim families and increased their hatred of the Serbs. When asked if she would ever return to her home, one women spoke for thousands of rape victims when she said, "Under no condition would I return to live in the same village with Serbs as before. I would never let my children go to a school with their children. I would not work with them. In fact, I would not even live in the same state with them." Her feelings underscore the difficulties of rebuilding relations between the peoples of the former Yugoslavia after the war. But though bitter memories of survivors pose obstacles to reconciliation, memory can also help to rebuild lives. As Francis Jones, a former student in Sarajevo, writes:

> It is important to keep faith with memory . . . for the sake of a land where memory may soon be all we have to cling to. Invaders down the ages have been drawn to conquest by Bosnia's rich upland pastures and the orchards of her valleys. Other enemies have burnt her fields, have put her villages to the knife or sword, and slaughtered her flocks. And yet, fields can be sown again, the blackened plum tree puts forth new shoots, the massacre's cowed survivors come down from their caves and build shacks from the rubble.

> But the new overlords are not content with conquest, with subjugation. They mean to obliterate a people; and they know full well that the most effective obliteration comes

from within, by setting neighbor against neighbor. But to wipe out a people, it is not enough to harry, to burn, and kill. Memory itself must be cleansed—memory that there ever was such a land, a land where the living was good, a land that all its people knew as home.

The ethnocide of the Bosnian Muslims and the enslavement of Bosnian women was designed to destroy and humiliate an entire population. Enslavement, which is a method of controlling people both mentally and physically, is a tactic that continues to be practiced in ethnic conflicts in some areas of the world.

Enslavement in Sudan

Today, slavery is being practiced in the North African country of Sudan, where it serves as the means by which northern Sudanese attempt to defeat a southern Sudanese independence movement and acquire southern territory. Sudan is divided ethnically into the northern territory, occupied mainly by Muslims, who are of Arab extraction, and the southern regions, peopled principally by Christians and animists (people who follow traditional African forms of nature worship), who are black. For thirteen years Muslim authorities in the north have attempted to impose Islamic law on the southern part of the country, while the southerners have fought for their autonomy.

Men lower a casket into the snow-covered ground of a Bosnian cemetery. As violence continues to sweep through Bosnia, cemeteries teem with the graves of genocide victims.

The borders of Sudan, the largest country in Africa, were drawn under Anglo-Egyptian colonial rule to include these different races, religions, and cultures. Britain considered separating the black non-Muslim African region in the southern Sudan from the Arab, Muslim north, but never carried out the plan. Sudan gained its independence from Britain in 1956, only after the north convinced the reluctant southern Sudanese that they would be granted representation in independent Sudan. But the northern Sudanese reneged on their promise and political power has remained concentrated in the north. The southern Sudanese now are fighting for independence and attempting to fend off northern Sudanese attempts to destroy their culture and people. These attempts include kidnapping and forced slavery.

Sudanese slave life

Thousands of southern black Sudanese have been abducted from their homes and sold into slavery. Some of them are children who are forced to serve as household servants, concubines, or field-workers for Sudanese Arabs. Others are confined in work camps and leased as property to private landowners. In 1989, a Dinka (a southern Sudanese tribe) woman or child slave could be purchased for ninety dollars; by 1990, an increase in the number of slave raids on Dinka villages had raised supply over demand, and the price of a Dinka slave fell to only fifteen dollars.

All of the slaves are stripped of their religious, cultural, and personal identities; they are stolen from their families and homes and given new identities as Muslims. Anti-Slavery International, an organization dedicated to the worldwide abolition of slavery, gathered the following report from an escaped child slave: "Kon, a thirteen-year-old Dinka boy, was abducted by Arab nomads and taken to a merchant's house. There he found several Dinka men hobbling, their Achilles tendons cut because they refused to become Muslims. Threatened with the same treatment, the boy converted."

Black children are rounded up and placed in secret government-run camps where they are instructed in Islam and forced not only to live as Muslims but also to fight against the resistance in the south. Boys as young as fifteen are pushed to the front lines where they are more likely to be shot. "They are virtually untrained; they are simply cannon fodder," says Gaspar Biro, the UN Special Rapporteur (reporter) on Human Rights in Sudan. Boys who managed to escape have testified that they were forced to donate blood to wounded northern Sudanese soldiers, a practice that can be fatal to underweight, malnourished youth.

A ravaged population

In addition to cultural and religious clashes, the civil war in Sudan has political and economic causes. The National Islamic Front (NIF) government wants control of all of Sudan, and is suspected of coveting the south's farmland and untapped oil reserves. According to the former deputy speaker of the Sudanese National Assembly, the northern government wants to repopulate the south with Muslims. "Slavery is a weapon that serves their political objective. Land is the prize." By forcing captives to become Muslims, and in some cases to fight against their own people, the Sudanese government is practicing ethnocide.

The civil war has orphaned tens of thousands of children who must find their own food and shelter. Southern Sudan also faces an enormous refugee crisis and famine. Operation Lifeline, a United Nations–led relief effort, estimates that only one-third of the original population in the south remains, and that the rest have either fled or died. The survival of southern Sudan's ethnic groups, among them the Dinka, Nuer, and Shilluk, is threatened. According to one relief worker, "The tragedy of southern Sudan is not the deaths. It is the number of people who have had to migrate and are treated like dirt—degraded, their culture taken away."

There are frequent reports that some of the Sudanese slaves are being exported to other North African and Persian Gulf countries. Many of the children are transported by truck to Libya, according to the U.S. embassy in Khartoum, the capital of Sudan. Slaves who are caught trying to escape are beaten, mutilated, or murdered. While the government of Sudan denies the existence of slavery within its borders, the firsthand testimony of escaped slaves indicates otherwise.

There has been almost no international protest against slavery in Sudan. Even African-American organizations, which so actively campaigned against apartheid in South Africa, have remained silent on this issue. Some African-American leaders, including Louis Farrakhan of the Nation of Islam, support the Islamic militancy of the northern Sudanese. Farrakhan refused the request of human rights worker Mohamed Athie of the International Coalition Against Chattel Slavery to speak about the crisis of slavery in Africa at the Million Man March in 1996. And the Congressional Black Caucus failed to back a resolution introduced by Congressman Barney Frank (D-MA) that would require the U.S. government to take action against slave-trading nations.

Cultural relativism

The existence of slavery in North Africa is rationalized by some as a cultural norm. In this era of multiculturalism, in which no one culture is supposed to be better than another, no one wants to point the finger at Islamic nations that condone slavery and say that what they are doing is wrong. Insistence within much of the international community on cultural relativism makes it difficult to criticize one cultural practice without implying that an entire culture is inferior to others. Slavery has been an aspect of Islamic culture for centuries; however, it is also a violation of human rights, as recognized by the United Nations, an international organization that is worldwide in scope and membership. The relativist argument defending religious and cultural tradition, however abhorrent, is the same one used to justify male dominance and discrimination against women, who in some countries are not allowed to vote or to express their opinions about practices affecting them. Regimes that repress ethnic groups and women often claim that members of their culture prefer the order im-

Children recently freed from slavery pose for a photograph during a conference on child servitude. Though slavery violates international human rights' laws, it has long been a component of Islamic culture.

posed by consensus to the disorder of political competition. As a result of these cultural differences, some governments believe that human rights standards should vary from country to country.

Finding ways to end the tension

Whenever an ethnic group feels that its rights are being curtailed, that group will typically attempt to fight back, either alone or with the help of foreign aid. Sometimes arbitration and intergroup dialogue can resolve such ethnic conflicts, while in severe cases it may be necessary to divide a state into ethnically homogeneous, autonomous units. If these efforts fail, persecuted groups may secede from a multiethnic state, may be driven out, or may be conquered and subsumed by a more powerful ethnic group. In recent years, the methods of resolving conflicts have often been the subject of as much scrutiny and controversy as are the problems that led to their implementation.

4

How Do Multiethnic States Attempt to Deal with Ethnic Conflict?

GROUPS IN MULTIETHNIC societies want prestige; they want their identity, language, culture, and traditions to be recognized. Ethnic groups also want access to a society's resources, which typically requires a substantial degree of influence and power. Economic and political conflicts are difficult to resolve, but certainly less difficult than issues of nationality, language, territorial homelands, and culture. As Samuel Huntington has written:

> Communists can become democrats, the rich can become poor and the poor rich, but Russians cannot become Estonians. . . . In class and ideological conflicts, the key question is "Which side are you on?" and people can and do change sides, but in conflicts between civilizations, the question is "What are you?" That is a given that cannot be changed.

Societies that experience ethnic conflict may have multiple social divisions along religious, class, political, and ethnic lines, making it difficult for negotiators to find room to compromise.

Multiethnic societies that experience ethnic conflicts and wish to resolve them must either manage the differences that lead to conflicts or, a much more drastic step, eliminate those differences. Means by which groups attempt to manage ethnic conflict include intergroup dialogue, arbitration, federalism, and hegemonic control. Methods of eliminating ethnic differences range from well-intentioned policies of assimilation to mass population transfers, secession, and even campaigns of genocide. Some of these tactics are self-serving and some are morally reprehensible, but all of them have been used at different times by people seeking to resolve conflicts of ethnic pluralism or to eliminate ethnic pluralism altogether.

Arbitrating ethnic differences

One of the most common methods of initiating ethnic conflict resolution is through dialogue and arbitration. By inviting spokespersons from each ethnicity in a multiethnic state to a discussion of differences, it may be possible to reach a compromise. Often quarreling groups within multiethnic states find it easier to ask a neutral third party to intervene and assist in the resolution of their differences. The role of the arbitrator is that of an outsider presiding over a family quarrel. The arbitrator, having no personal stake in the conflict, can take the interests of the rival groups into account and present a set of compromises that may win the support of both sides.

One of the issues that often turns up at the center of group conflicts in multiethnic societies is language. Because language is the bearer of ethnic and cultural tradition, it is important symbolically and practically to each ethnic group. Each group may want its language rights respected, or given official status. When groups have agreed to compromise on the issue of language, the result has been improved relations between ethnic groups. In Switzerland, the meeting place of three major and other minor European language groups, Italian, French, German, and Romansh speakers all get along thanks to intergroup dialogue and mutual respect, which has traditionally included Swiss willingness to learn one another's languages. However, dialogue and arbitration are only useful when all sides are willing to sit down and discuss their grievances in a constructive way. If groups cannot compromise on the issue of language, for example, language loyalties and ethnic backgrounds may become the basis for separatist movements that threaten the sovereignty of the state. This has been the case in Canada, where an upsurge in ethnic conflict between Native Americans and French and British Canadians in recent years has been attributed to the removal of an imperial arbitrator from England who had worked to resolve conflicts in the provinces and territories until 1982, when Canada ceased to be a British dominion. French-speaking Quebecois, in particular, demand the official use of French and have used the French language as the rallying point for their separatist movement. If ethnic groups fail to arbitrate their differences or reach compromise through dialogue, the likelihood that they will be able to share power within the state decreases.

Power sharing

Power sharing is a method of ethnic conflict regulation that can only succeed when rival ethnic groups are willing to make concessions. Power sharing can be a powerful tool for dealing with ethnically motivated conflicts. If

Members of the French separatist movement demonstrate during a parade in Montreal, Quebec, where a power struggle between Native Americans and British and French Canadians has consumed the province.

leaders, recognizing the ethnic pluralism of their society, can sit down before elections and make deals that promise defeated parties a voice in national politics, whatever the election results, conflicts can be reduced. When people of various interests are assured representation in their government, numerically weaker ethnic groups need not fear a winner-take-all election.

In Belgium, power sharing has helped ease tensions between Dutch-speaking Flemings and French-speaking Walloons. The economic dominance of the Flemings, who chafe at subsidizing the poorer Walloons, is one source of the conflict. Separatist movements exist among both groups, but they have managed to coexist under Belgium's federal constitution, which allows all groups representation in government.

The most humane approach

Power sharing can also involve an agreement that no one religion may become more powerful than any other through state subsidies. In some cases, different ethnic groups can avoid conflicts by agreeing to separate religious institutions from politics. Countries such as Belgium, Lebanon, and the Netherlands have successfully managed to keep church and state separate. This also helps assure citizens that they will not be persecuted or ignored because of their spiritual beliefs. When one religion receives recognition from the state while others do not, ethnic conflicts can arise. This has been the case in predominantly Protestant Northern Ireland, where discrimination against Catholics has resulted in violence. However, strict separation of church and state can also work against conflict resolution: In Egypt, Muslim fundamentalists have waged a terrorist campaign against the nonsectarian government that does not promote Islam (or any other religion).

According to *Foreign Policy* editor William Maynes, "Power sharing is the most humane approach to the problem of ethnic conflict, but . . . as John Stuart Mill pronounced in *Representative Government*, democracy is 'next to impossible' in a country with a multiethnic population." In countries with majority and minority populations, it may be difficult to apportion representation equally. Some groups, by virtue of their numbers, will be more powerful than others. If ethnic groups fail to arrive at a fair method of sharing power, then these groups may choose to divide up their nation into ministates with more or less exclusive political power over their own affairs. This process is known as federalism.

Federalism

Regional ethnic groups may be appeased by setting up a system of federalism—that is, by partitioning the state into mini–political units, each of which has political power. Federalism can work in a society where ethnic communities are clustered geographically, since federations can be created out of these identifiable units. Federalism has succeeded, for example, in Belgium, where ethnic groups are clustered geographically into Dutch-speaking Flanders, French-speaking Flanders, and bilingual Brussels.

However, federalism failed to prevent trouble in Yugoslavia between Serbs, Croats, and Bosnian Muslims. According to one political scientist, "Federalism proved totally insufficient as a conflict-regulating device in Yugoslavia because there was insufficient geographical clustering of the relevant ethnic communities." Croats, Serbs, and Bosnian Muslims were integrated throughout the former Yugoslavia, rather than clustered in ethnic enclaves. Their integration continues to create problems today, as Bosnian refugees attempt to return to their homes, side by side with the Serbs whose aggressiveness sparked the forty-three-month war in Bosnia. In April 1996, ethnic violence again erupted between Bosnian refugees trying to return home and Serbs who attempted to block their way. Under the 1995 Dayton Accord, more than two million people displaced from their homes by war in Bosnia are entitled to return to their place of origin. However, few refugees have been able to cross the boundary line between Bosnia's Muslim-Croat federation and its Serb land. According to a North Atlantic Treaty Organization (NATO) spokesman, "If Bosnia cannot function as a multiethnic democracy envisioned under the Dayton plan, then it will be partitioned into ethnic ministates." However, given the heterogeneous makeup of prewar Bosnia, partitioning Bosnia into distinct ethnic states will be nearly impossible. When populations are not cleanly divided, and too many groups in one region call for autonomy based on their ethnic identity, the given region may not be able to unify under federalist principles. One of the reasons why Serbs, Bosnian Muslims, and Croats existed peacefully under the former Yugoslavia was because of the domination of the Soviet government, which successfully suppressed ethnic uprisings through the threat of Soviet retaliation.

Hegemonic control

Although not a popular solution in today's world, control wielded by a dictatorship, authoritarian regime, or empire is capable of suppressing ethnic conflict through outright domination. Such influential power is known as hegemonic control. The Soviet Union was an example of an authoritarian regime that successfully suppressed ethnic tensions, because, essentially, people were more afraid of the government than of each other. As Charles William

In Sarajevo, the multiethnic capital of Bosnia, residents retrieve water from a public fountain. Before the war, Serbs, Croats, and Muslims lived side-by-side in the heterogeneous city; now, as refugees try to return to their homes, ethnic conflicts arise between former neighbors.

Maynes has noted, however, repression "is an answer that provides a temporary solution today but prepares the way for a political explosion tomorrow. Those repressed only await the day when they can rise up." This was evident in 1991 when the collapse of the Soviet Union led to an upsurge in ethnic and nationalist conflicts that had lain dormant for decades.

Hegemonic control, arbitration, power sharing, and federalism are all means by which states attempt to manage ethnic conflict. Some governments, however, actively promote ethnic conflict in situations where it may help them accomplish their goals.

Manipulating ethnic conflict

Some governments, rather than seeking to resolve ethnic conflicts, actually try to turn their ethnic populations against each other. These governments believe that ethnic conflicts will further their own interests. Ethnic conflicts provide the ideal opportunity for politicians interested in creating or dividing political constituencies. In the 1970s, trade union membership on the Caribbean islands of Trinidad and Tobago was based on ethnicity, as industries themselves were organized along ethnic lines. In the past, broad repression under a common foe had brought ethnic groups together; however, efforts at cooperation between

Demonstrators in favor of a democratic Soviet Union rally in Moscow. The authoritarian regime finally collapsed in 1991, paving the way for increased ethnic and nationalist conflicts.

rural-based East Indian sugar workers and the urban-based nonimmigrant mine workers were discouraged by the government of Trinidad and Tobago. When the miners went on strike in solidarity with Indian sugar workers striking for higher wages, the government retaliated against leaders of the Mine Workers Union, and most lost their jobs. By punishing the mostly black mine workers, the government hoped to turn blacks against Indians, thereby preventing any further collusion between them. By its action, the Trinidadian government hoped to create ethnic tensions to prevent two groups, blacks and Indians, from succeeding through cooperation. This behavior is similar to that of the Soviets, who, in their nationality policies, settled antagonistic ethnic groups together with the hope that internal discord would inhibit the groups from ever collaborating to overthrow the state.

If they do not wish to manipulate or manage ethnic conflict, some governments may attempt to eliminate the source of ethnic conflict altogether by making a state ethnically homogeneous. One of the most common methods of eliminating ethnic differences is through assimilation.

Assimilation

Forming diverse groups into a common civic and patriotic or ethnic identity is one method of eliminating differences. By nation building, a state attempts to create a distinctive, inclusive identity for its citizens. Conforming to this national identity is known as assimilation, or integration. According to political scientists John McGarry and Brendan O'Leary:

> Integrationists favor policies which reduce the differences between communities, ensuring that the children of the (potentially rival) communities go to the same schools, socializing them in the same language and conventions, [and] encouraging public and private housing policies which prevent segregation.

Some policies go further, however, and encourage the merging of ethnic identities into an already established identity or a new identity. In France, for example, new immigrants have been encouraged to take on the French

This 1886 photograph is a dramatic example of the assimilation of Native Americans. In an effort to integrate these Apache teens into white society, they were forced to cut their hair and give up their traditional attire. Opponents argue that assimilation is another form of ethnocide.

identity. When one community adopts the culture of the dominant community, assimilation may be considered a form of ethnocide (the destruction of a culture). Indigenous communities around the world have raised this objection when the dominant culture's language, religion, or culture was given preference in the process of assimilation. Many Native American groups, for example, feel they have been assimilated into a majority culture that reflects nothing of their heritage. Although it seeks to resolve ethnic conflict by eliminating differences, assimilation ignores an important issue, which is the desire of members of ethnic communities to maintain their differences. When conflicting national and ethnic communities each seek the right to self-determination, secession may resolve the conflict by allowing a separation of communities.

Secession

Breaking up multiethnic states into separate communities can resolve conflicts by allowing the separation of ethnic groups that do not want to be a part of the same nation. An ethnic group may be motivated to seek self-determination because it has been discriminated against, or a threatened minority population may seek independence as a means of preserving its ethnic culture from extinction. Groups may secede in the hope of finding greater economic and political freedom, increased power and prestige, and the ability to create their own public policy.

Since the collapse of the Soviet Union and Yugoslavia in 1991, secession has been the dominant method of ethnic conflict resolution in Europe. As the secession of Czechs and Slovaks from the former Czechoslovakia in 1993 suggests, peaceful secession is possible in the post–cold war world. However, the bloody and protracted war between Chechnya and Russia, from which Chechnya seeks to secede, is an example of how violent secessionist conflicts can become.

"The difficulty with partition," writes *Foreign Policy* editor Charles William Maynes, "is that the line cannot be drawn with any exactitude. Significant minorities will be left behind. New ones will be exposed or develop. Partition has been impossible in Bosnia-Herzegovina because the Croatian, Muslim, and Serbian populations have been so mixed."

As former British foreign secretary Geoffrey Howe notes, secession can create problems not only for nations as a whole, but also for individual citizens who may have divided loyalties.

> Of course every person, every people has the right to preserve their language, culture, communication, faith and traditions. Of course these specific rights must be safeguarded.

Secessionist movements are prone to become violent ethnic conflicts. Here, heavily armed Chechen rebels prepare to battle their Russian counterparts.

But to say that is certainly not to call for the establishment of an autonomous state for each nation, each ethnic group, each tribe. Indeed, demands of such an absolutist kind can actively impede, positively frustrate, the safeguarding of people's actual rights. Consider, for example, the situation of partners in an ethnically mixed marriage or family in a state which is being broken up, divided on ethnic lines. When a person in such circumstances, as has all too often happened, faces the need to choose between nation and family, surely he is being confronted with an immoral choice?

Another problem with secession is that it can create a domino effect whereby ethnic minorities within seceding territories in turn seek their own self-determination. In addition, secession raises the issue of what territory a seceding group may claim as its own. This can be a delicate issue, especially in areas where mixed populations have lived in close proximity. If populations are not cleanly divided, mass population transfers may be enforced by an authoritarian government that wants to create ethnically homogeneous territories.

Mass population transfers

One of the most dramatic methods of eliminating ethnic differences is the mass transfer of an entire ethnic population from its home. In a process that seeks to remove unwanted ethnic groups, a population is pushed back to its alleged "homeland" or transported to a new location. Targeted communities can be evicted from the state or moved internally, as was the case with Stalin's infamous internal deportations. In 1944 the Soviet dictator forced the Chechen and Ingush people from their homelands in the northern Caucasus and marched them to Siberia and Kazakhstan. The peoples of the Caucasus had been a chronic nuisance to the Soviet state, resisting all attempts at state-planned development in their region, and revolting on numerous occasions. They were deported internally in an attempt to prevent them from rebelling again. Their uprooting and relocation caused massive loss of life and nearly eliminated much of the culture and many of the customs of these ancient peoples. Population transfers are

"Sorry, but these organs seem to reject your body."

a form of ethnocide, since the intent is to kill a culture by taking away its homeland and destroying its roots. In addition to the Chechens and Ingush, Stalin internally deported the Meskhetian Turks, relocating them in the Central Asian republics, where they experienced ethnic discrimination and persecution that resulted in their evacuation from the region in 1989.

Population transfers displace ethnic conflicts, but they do not resolve them. According to the journal *Parliamentary Affairs*, "Current outrages in the northern Caucasus can be traced directly to Stalin's displacements of peoples, some of whom have returned to reclaim their homes." In 1957, when Communist Party general secretary Nikita Khrushchev allowed those who had been deported internally to return to their territories, Chechens returned on foot to reclaim their ancestral homeland. Their return resulted in the displacement of other peoples who had been settled in Chechnya by the Soviet government. Disputes over who has claim to this land were a central cause of the war between Russia and Chechnya that began in 1995. Population transfers cause massive social upheavals that take years to resolve. The aftermath of mass population transfers has created at least 164 territorial disputes among ethnic groups in the former Soviet Union. These ethnic tensions have forced more than eight million people in Chechnya and elsewhere in the former Soviet Union to abandon their homes since 1989.

Forced mass transfers of people have occurred throughout history between competing ethnic groups. In North America, Native Americans were forced off ancestral lands under pressure from the early colonists, and in the nineteenth century the U.S. government instituted the forced resettlement program to so-called Indian reservations.

The Jews of Europe were victims of forced population transfers at the hands of the Nazis. In the 1970s, Turkey expelled Greek Cypriots from Cyprus, and Idi Amin, dictator of Uganda, expelled Uganda's prosperous Asian community. If, however, a population transfer does not have the desired effect, a regime may use stronger measures to accomplish its goals.

Genocide

The elimination of an ethnic group is accomplished through a practice known as genocide. Genocide is the mass killing of a race or *genos* (kind), but the same effect—the elimination of an unwanted population—can be accomplished by persecuting a group until it cannot sustain itself, or by imposing birth control on the subject group. Genocide depends on a racial, ethnic, or religious ideology that supports a nonuniversalist conception of human beings—that is, the idea that some people have more rights than others. This belief allows many who carry out mass murder to justify their actions.

The past century alone has seen many instances of genocide. In 1915, thousands of Turkish Armenian men, women, and children were shot, hanged, and starved to death by ethno-nationalist Turks who did not want Armenians in Turkey. In Germany, the Nazis committed genocide against Jews, Gypsies, Poles, and Russians in the 1930s and 1940s.

Genocide was committed in the Soviet Union against an estimated seven million Ukrainians who starved to death during the 1932–33 famines created by the collectivization policies of Stalin. Stalin's agricultural programs, in which private farms were seized and turned into farming cooperatives in which workers received no personal benefit for their efforts, were designed to undermine the independence of farmers and destroy Ukrainian nationalism. Such drastic and ill-managed changes resulted in disastrous crop failures, confusion, mass terror, and violence against farmers. The Stalin-engineered famines also caused half the population of Kazakhstan, then a Soviet Central Asian republic, to starve during the first wave of collectivization from 1929 to 1931.

More recently, in Cambodia in the 1970s communist dictator Pol Pot waged a campaign of genocide against anyone not of "pure" Khmer stock, and his policies claimed the lives of one and a half million Chinese, Vietnamese, Laotian, Thai, Indian, and Pakistani people. Pol Pot also attempted to eradicate religion from Cambodia and killed so many Buddhist priests that their population plunged from sixty thousand to thirty thousand within four years.

The twenty-five million Kurds who constitute the Middle East's fourth-largest ethnic group have been the victims of genocide in Iraq, where leader Saddam Hussein views them as an undesirable minority. In the 1980s Kurds became the objects of an Iraqi genocidal campaign that included forced relocation programs for Kurds and the gassing of Kurdish villages.

Genocide is intended to end ethnic conflict, and it usually results in the acquisition of land for the victors. "Yet," write scholars John McGarry and Brendan O'Leary, "genocides often fail to achieve their objectives, and always create explosive and historically entrenched

This pile of human skulls and bones serves as a grim reminder of Communist dictator Pol Pot's genocidal reign in Cambodia during the 1970s.

bitterness and fear amongst the descendants of victims." The Jews will never forget the memory of the Holocaust, in which two-thirds of their population in Europe was exterminated. More than eighty years later, the Armenians are still the enemies of the Turks. Bosnian Serbs and Muslims, who bear the scars of genocide and civil war, will have difficulty rebuilding relations.

The survivors of genocide and other forms of oppression often look to international security institutions to intervene in ethnic conflicts and, afterward, to assist in rehabilitation. When international organizations should intervene, and in what circumstances, are subjects of much debate. With few exceptions, the world community has increasingly refused to ignore blatant human rights violations, and intervention in situations where human rights are not being respected is more likely now than it was in the past.

5

Foreign Intervention
in Ethnic Conflicts

THE WEST IS currently at an extraordinary peak of power. The USSR, its lone superpower opponent, has ceased to exist, and Western military power knows no rivals. Yet according to former Central Intelligence Agency (CIA) director James Woolsey, the world is "more dangerous" now than during the cold war because it is bombarded with ethnic, nationalist, and separatist conflicts that threaten world security. Ethnic conflicts have occurred throughout history; however, as David Callahan, project director of the Twentieth Century Fund, points out:

> The huge increase in ethnic violence during recent years has left many observers wondering where it will end. Is the world at the beginning of a long cycle of ethnic conflict, or will some plateau of stability be reached in the next few years? No clear answer to this question exists, yet undoubtedly there is the potential for enormous violence.

When ethnic conflict leads to humanitarian disaster, critics often charge that international intervention could have prevented the crisis. For example, Mohamed Sahnoun, former head of the UN mission in Somalia, believes there were several opportunities for early intervention that could have prevented the anarchy and civil war that finally prompted international intervention in that country in 1992. Early action can be very effective in handling ethnic conflict, but once conflict reaches the violence stage, intervention is much more difficult.

An armed UN vehicle passes through a war-ravaged section of Mogadishu, Somalia. The United Nations has been criticized for not responding sooner to the crisis in Somalia; critics contend that early intervention could have prevented the bloody civil war.

The level of tragedy associated with ethnic violence, combined with round-the-clock media coverage, generates public pressure on the United Nations and powerful nations like the United States to intervene in conflicts after they have become destructive. However, intervention in ethnic conflicts, particularly after they have become violent, usually presents a no-win situation to policymakers, as attempts to stop the conflict can lead to even more problems. Late intervention is rarely easy. Ethnic conflicts are complicated and they provide no clearly drawn battle lines. U.S. secretary of state Warren Christopher repeatedly referred to the Bosnian conflict as "a problem from hell" because every attempt to reduce the conflict after it exploded seemed to present an array of new problems. While the public and the media pressured the Western world to stop the ethnic violence, policymakers were aware that an extreme measure such as committing troops might quickly erode public support for intervention in Bosnia. Similarly, a UN embargo that prohibited outside arms shipments to Bosnia raised an outcry from critics who believed it only hurt the Bosnian Muslims by crippling their effort to defend themselves against Serbian aggression.

While embargoes are intended to disable conflicts by prohibiting the sale of arms, they often fail because of the proliferation of illegal and smuggled arms. Supplying arms to a conflict is a commonly employed intervention strategy. Throughout history powerful states have contributed weapons to a favored side of an ethnic conflict, in an attempt to help it overcome its opposition. According to one analyst of ethnic conflicts, "Tribal warriors confront each other in these wars with weapons they acquire, directly or indirectly, from their well-wishers . . . or client seekers elsewhere in the world."

Arming foreign conflicts

During the cold war, the United States and the USSR, the two superpowers, each sought allies, particularly in the nonaligned, developing world. The Soviets sent arms to assist developing nations in Marxist uprisings that would ally them with the USSR. The United States sent arms to groups that were willing to fight the Communists, and rewarded countries that remained democratic, recruiting them for the Western side in the balance of power.

Superpowers have historically supported the side of an ethnic conflict which best promotes their own interest by arming and aiding that faction and helping it to remain on top. The Soviet invasion of Afghanistan in 1979 was undertaken with the goal of bolstering Soviet power in that country. In response, the United States supplied arms to the Muslim nationalist resistance force in Afghanistan, known as the mujahideen. The United States also attempted to block communist expansion in places like Vietnam and Latin America by supporting anticommunist factions, which were often also ethnic factions.

Some critics charge that arming foreign conflicts is nothing more than an attempt to exert imperialist power over the affairs of another nation. U.S. foreign policy critic Ngugi Wa Thiong'o has referred to the U.S. role in arming foreign conflicts as "neo-colonial control . . . that takes the particular form of erecting and supporting the most reactionary and the most repressive civil or military dictatorships in the world . . . for as long as they guarantee the continued dominance of U.S.A. interests."

The United Nations works to maintain international stability with the hope that peace and security will promote global demilitarization and arms reduction. As the chief means of maintaining international peace, the United Nations is frequently called upon to intervene in ethnic conflicts.

The role of the United Nations

The United Nations, an international organization representing 185 countries, has the primary purpose of maintaining international peace and security. Founded at the end of World War II, the goals of the organization were laid out in its charter: "To save succeeding generations from the scourge of war . . . to reaffirm faith in fundamental human rights, . . . to establish conditions under which justice and respect for the obligations arising from treaties and other sources of international law can be maintained, and to promote social progress and better standards of life in larger freedom." The new, more volatile political climate that emerged at the end of the cold war has challenged the UN's established practices and policies regarding conflict resolution.

The United Nations is frequently pressured to resolve ethnic conflicts out of humanitarian concerns or out of fear that the conflict will escalate into an ever-widening regional war. Appeals to the UN for peacemaking purposes have skyrocketed in recent years, calling into question the UN goal of collective security, by which each member's security is supposed to be ensured by all. The UN cannot intervene in every ethnic conflict around the globe, but some critics charge that intervention in one area and not another is hypocritical. Others believe the impossibility of acting everywhere should not prevent the UN from acting anywhere.

Representatives from around the world meet during a session of the United Nations, an organization that comprises 185 member countries and works to maintain international peace.

The frequent demands by member states for collective military action and humanitarian intervention to deal with ethnic conflicts requires that the UN play a larger role in international crises than ever before in its history. The number of UN operations launched since 1988 alone surpasses the total number of operations for the first forty years of its existence. Since 1990, UN peacekeeping forces—comprised of delegates and soldiers from the member nations—have performed a variety of duties, from monitoring elections in Nicaragua, Eritrea, and Cambodia to encouraging peace negotiations in Angola, Bosnia, and El Salvador to distributing food in Somalia and Bosnia.

Military intervention

UN peacekeeping forces are placed in situations where they work to contain conflicts, usually after all sides have been pressured to negotiate a cease-fire. The troops are to remain neutral and use force only in self-defense. In Bosnia, UN peacekeeping troops from the NATO alliance were authorized to use force if necessary to protect UN convoy vehicles, setting an important precedent.

Gathering and organizing the troops can be problematic and time-consuming because member nations have to willingly donate forces to an operation that has been agreed upon by the UN. Citing the lack of an international security force, former secretary-general Boutros Boutros-Ghali called for the creation of a standing UN force, a body that could be immediately dispatched to control outbreaks of violence. Analysts concur that the threat of military intervention must be backed up by a body of force. Punitive measures are necessary to enforce international law. The safety of UN peacekeeping forces is often an issue when committing troops to ethnically torn areas. Peacekeepers can become hostages, even victims. Public support for military intervention, which inevitably puts troops in harm's way, may dissolve when lives are lost in distant, poorly understood conflicts.

Military intervention also runs the risk of upsetting the local population of the troubled nation. And lengthy

A frightened Somali woman runs for cover as U.S. Army helicopters pass overhead. Although military intervention may help resolve ethnic conflicts, the strong foreign presence may be upsetting for the local population.

engagements in foreign countries can arouse unpopular sentiment among the citizens of the intervening nation. Occasionally the purpose of a military presence can backfire and lead to embarrassing situations for the intervening nations.

Intervention in Somalia

In 1992 and 1993, over twenty thousand UN peacekeeping troops from twenty-nine countries were sent to Somalia to protect the delivery of food to that nation's starving population. Somalia's government had been racked by strife among ethnic factions since gaining independence in 1960, and by the 1990s competing political and paramilitary organizations based on clan identity were attempting to overthrow the predominantly Darood (a Somali clan) military regime. The different contingents of UN peacekeepers disagreed over how to solve Somalia's problems. The U.S. contingent argued that in order to secure the distribution of food, it would be necessary to arrest the Somali leader, Mohammed Aidid. This new offensive role of U.S. soldiers led to violence and civilian casualties, which other peacekeepers believed only broadened the war. Speaking on the effect of the U.S. actions, the Italian chief of staff in Somalia, General Domenico Corcione, said, "A peace mission is being transformed into a war operation." In response to civilian casualties, angry Somali citizens overpowered and killed U.S. servicemen and dragged them through the streets of Mogadishu, the Somali capital. The humiliation generated resentment in the United States for the government's mishandling of the crisis. It forced policymakers and peacekeeping forces to recognize that they had been naive in believing a humanitarian operation could intervene successfully in Somalia. The real lack in Somalia was order, not food, and restoring order required that the intervening nations provide a more involved military presence than many of them were prepared to provide.

Because of its military and diplomatic power, the United States, more so than any other country, is often pressured to become involved in ethnic conflicts around the globe.

U.S. intervention in foreign conflicts

During the cold war, U.S. foreign policy toward nationalist movements and ethnic conflicts was shaped by concerns such as the desire to stop the spread of communism. Since 1991, U.S. foreign policy has had to accommodate the ideal of helping nations become self-determined and the need to protect U.S. interests. The lessons of the Vietnam War, in which military intervention abroad led to prolonged involvement, massive casualties, and failure to achieve any clear objectives, produced a cautious approach in U.S. foreign policy. Officials came to see the desirability of using military force to intervene in foreign conflicts only when U.S. vital interests were threatened and when success could be guaranteed. However, that policy leaves little flexibility in dealing with ethnic conflicts abroad.

Policymakers have sought options in intervention between doing nothing and embarking on full-scale military action. The search for middle ground has resulted in collective action, in which the United States, along with other UN member nations, contributes some money and troops to a peacekeeping force but does not take full responsibility for an operation. Critics of collective action argue that international organizations like the UN lack the power to enforce their threats and that the UN must back up threats with punitive action or member states will be unwilling to become involved in operations. According to Amnesty International's report on human rights for 1994:

> The lesson [policymakers must learn] is not the futility of collective action, but the importance of justice remaining central to the cause. Until the rule of law is understood as essential to peace, until the end to murder and torture is seen as lying in accountability rather than accommodation, the growing number of states willing to join a collective defense will remain insufficient to secure respect for human rights.

The human tragedies of ethnic cleansing in Bosnia, and the deadly retaliation the Muslims sometimes delivered, led the United States to intervene with diplomatic and humanitarian efforts. However, until 1994 the United States was reluctant to take any stronger action in the UN-led operation, largely because Bosnia was not deemed vital to American interests.

Vital interests

Defense Secretary William Perry defines a "vital interest" literally and broadly, as one that affects the country's "national survival." The United States fought the Persian Gulf War to liberate Kuwait, which had been invaded by Iraq. Kuwait's status as a petroleum-exporting country certainly affected U.S. attitudes toward its safety. The United States does not want to experience another energy crisis like the one precipitated by the oil embargo of the Organization of Petroleum Exporting Countries (OPEC) in the 1970s.

Choosing when and where to intervene in conflicts based on their significance to U.S. interests is realist foreign policy. Yet realist policy often seems hypocritical. For example, the United States continues to provide foreign aid to the Kurdish minority in the U.S.-created safe haven zone in northern Iraq. U.S. aid helps to ensure that the Kurdish minority is protected, but it also assures the continued U.S. presence in that oil-rich part of the world. Yet the United States has done nothing to help persecuted Kurds in Turkey or to halt the conflict there between the government and Turkey's rebel Kurds, who are also a persecuted ethnic minority. This is realist policy at work; since the United States cannot intervene in every conflict around the globe, it chooses first those which are vital to its own safety or economic stability.

Although the war in Bosnia was not politically or economically of vital interest to the United States, its outcome and aftermath relates to the United States in important philosophical ways. Warren Zimmerman, former U.S. ambassador to Yugoslavia, declared the war in Bosnia to have "baleful [potentially very bad] implications for the United States" because what is at stake there are "the values of the melting pot." If failed states and divided societies cannot be repaired they will be cited by some as evidence that the American democratic notions of tolerance and pluralism cannot be applied abroad. These ideals rest on the assumption that reasonable people will be willing to compromise, to reason, and to make concessions. However, ethnic, nationalist, and secessionist conflicts are usually the result of an unwillingness or a failure to make compromises.

Iraqi Kurds wash clothes in a refugee camp. By providing aid to the persecuted Kurds, the United States is able to maintain a powerful presence in the oil-bearing country of Iraq.

Middle-ground foreign policy

From the crisis in the Balkans, there developed a U.S. foreign policy that embraces the idealist rhetoric of self-determination but leans toward what can realistically be accomplished without becoming too involved. Influenced by public distress at U.S. inaction in the face of atrocities in Bosnia, President Bill Clinton called for NATO ultimatums. NATO air power against the Serbs was employed in the spring of 1994.

This policy switch did not reflect a new belief that peace in Bosnia was vital to U.S. security; rather, it was due to increased sympathy for Bosnians among the American people based on continuous media coverage of the outrages against Bosnia's Muslims, particularly Serb attacks on UN-designated safe havens and the mortar attack on civilians in a marketplace in Sarajevo, the Bosnian capital, in February 1994. President Clinton responded to the humanitarian impulses of Americans with a strategy of limited intervention that kept the risk of American embroilment at a minimum, thereby finding a middle ground between realist and idealist foreign policy aims.

Ignoring Rwanda

In contrast, the American reaction to atrocities and ethnic cleansing in Rwanda in 1994 was less intense. When members of the Hutu ethnic group began a genocidal campaign to expunge Tutsis as well as moderate Hutus, the international community was slow to react. Unlike the conflict in Bosnia, which unfolded over time and was covered extensively by the media, exposing Americans to the horrors of the war, the outburst of ethnic violence in Rwanda occurred suddenly, and media coverage at the time was limited. Although the Rwandan genocide was on a much larger scale, the United States was slow to react to the crisis. Comparing the reaction to atrocities in Bosnia and Rwanda, one expert on U.S. foreign policy and ethnic conflicts said, "A genocidal campaign in Europe, in a country with modern cities like Sarajevo, seemed more disturbing than massacres of a far greater dimension on a continent where vast human suffering is a common occurrence."

Under what circumstances is one country justified in interfering in the affairs of another to protect an endangered minority? The desire to protect human rights, particularly those of minority groups, often interferes with the sovereignty of states.

Protecting human rights

Promoting respect for human rights, which is the idea that all people, because they are human, have certain inalienable rights to life and liberty, is one of the principal objectives of the United Nations. The UN Commission on Human Rights is concerned with issues such as freedom of opinion and peaceful assembly, freedom from slavery and arbitrary arrest, as well as women's rights, children's rights, labor laws, and racial discrimination. In 1992 the UN General Assembly adopted a resolution on minority rights stating that minorities had the right to practice their culture, religion, and language.

However, many states, particularly those in the developing world, fear that the developed countries will use human rights as an excuse to exert control over their affairs. The concept of human rights is not universally accepted, and standards of rights vary from country to country. Yet the international community as represented by the United Nations holds to the belief that all people are entitled to the same basic rights.

The whole world is watching

When persecuted groups want to bring their situation to the attention of others, they can now contact the international media, gaining worldwide sympathy and sometimes direct support. Indeed, the communications revolution has challenged state sovereignty, as a growing international

A UN representative meets with Sudanese refugees during a visit to Africa. The United Nations is dedicated to protecting persecuted minorities and to defending human rights.

consciousness of and concern for internal conflicts and persecuted peoples have called into question the idea that states have the right to manage their internal affairs.

Ethnic conflicts are now televised. Photojournalists and news reporters have the power to turn the tide of public opinion and compel political action when they bring scenes of atrocities from around the world into the living rooms of America. Foreign policy decisions are increasingly driven by photographs—images of genocide in Rwanda, starving children in Somalia, tortured prisoners of war in Bosnia, Kurdish refugees in Iraq. The revolution in global telecommunications may serve to make the world not only more aware of conflicts in far-flung reaches of the world, but also more willing to respond in these matters. Many believe that without continuous coverage of Serb atrocities against Bosnian Muslims, it is unlikely that the United States would have authorized the intervention of NATO forces. The news media have helped to show the world when and where there may be a need for international intervention. Without the information supplied by journalists and news networks, many violent conflicts would play themselves out, unscrutinized and unaccountable to world opinion.

Foreign intervention in the domestic affairs of other nations, however, is often a difficult and slow process. Unless member countries offer military support, the United Nations lacks the means to enforce its threats. The difficulty of enforcing international law is evident in the workings of the UN war crimes tribunal, which has attempted to hold individuals responsible for crimes committed during times of war.

The UN war crimes tribunal

The United Nations is dedicated to defending the human rights of minority groups and other persecuted peoples, as well as making the perpetrators of crimes against humanity accountable for their actions. Part of its function is the development of international law, and it has codified, or systematically organized, laws pertaining to crimes committed during times of war. Crimes of war include any act of aggression, annexation of territory, genocide, and the systematic use of rape as an instrument of war. These kinds of international laws were applied to accused Nazi war criminals at a famous series of trials held in Nuremberg, Germany, in 1950. The UN Security Council set up a similar war crimes tribunal in February 1993 to deal with the atrocities committed in the conflict in Bosnia-Herzegovina. The tribunal is supposed to indict (charge) and prosecute those accused of responsibility for crimes such as rape, torture, execution, punitive starvation, and the shelling of civilians and peacekeepers. Those found guilty will be punished according to the rules of international law.

Bosnia's tribunal

The Bosnian War Crimes Tribunal, which is the largest investigation project of its kind since the Nuremberg trials, has gathered masses of evidence. Its computerized database of videotapes, photographs, and documents includes statements from thousands of people that give detailed information on mass graves, prison camps, and paramilitary groups. However, the tribunal lacks the power to arrest, and it has no police force. It relies on governments to seize and turn over suspects. The tribunal's inability to enforce its laws has been criticized. "To have a body of humanitarian law, built up over decades and accepted by the great majority of UN member states, without an enforcement mechanism is a fruitless exercise," says South African judge Richard Goldstone, who is known for his investigations of political violence. "The success of this tribunal will be a powerful argument for creating a permanent international criminal court. . . . Its failure will be a step away from that goal." The tribunal has also been criticized within the United Nations because some members are wary of creating a body that has the power to investigate crimes committed within their own states. Other member states fear that the tribunal's work might obstruct peace negotiations in nations like the former Yugoslavia.

Despite rampant criticism and complaints, a similar war crimes tribunal has been set in place by the Security Council to examine the charges against those accused of perpetrating violence in Rwanda in 1994. Methods of dealing with ethnic violence are highly debated, but many world leaders agree that in order to deal with conflicts effectively, it is first necessary to have an understanding of how the problems were created.

Understanding ethnic conflict

How to approach ethnic conflict remains a central issue for today's leaders, for as Richard Schulz, director of the International Security Studies Program at Tufts University, writes:

> Ethnic and religious conflicts are and will be among the main determinants of regional disorder in the coming years. They are the source for much of the internal war and ungovernability that now affect an increasing number of states. An understanding of these developments is essential for the international community if it is to undertake conflict resolution and post-conflict reconstruction assistance of these fractured states.

An understanding of how conflicts are created, together with strong diplomatic measures to prevent disputes from escalating into violence, may help to prevent and contain ethnic violence. Although conflicts that have already exploded in violence may necessitate military intervention, it is possible to intervene on behalf of ethnic conflicts before they become violent. Monitoring and early action are among the diplomatic methods that aim to prevent ethnic violence.

6

Preventing Ethnic Violence

"A DEFINING CHARACTERISTIC of the post–Cold War era has been the disjuncture between its complex, horrifying events—anarchy in Somalia, civil war in the former Yugoslavia, genocide in Rwanda—and the presumption among some foreign policy elites that easy solutions to such disasters can be found," says Stephen John Stedman, professor of comparative politics at Johns Hopkins School of International Studies. Establishing policy on preventing ethnic conflicts is a central challenge for post–cold war strategists. According to Leslie Gelb, president of the Council on Foreign Relations, "The main strategic challenge for the United States is to develop plans . . . to stem civil wars." The principles to guide these new policies are derived by analyzing the successes and failures of the past to determine what methods will be most effective in handling future crises.

Some analysts believe ethnic violence can be avoided with a threefold policy of prediction, prevention, and intervention. The key to preventing conflicts lies in being able to predict when they are likely to occur so an effective plan can be put in place to stop them. Not every ethnically divided state erupts in violence. Drawing on experience, policymakers can develop a method for identifying high-risk from low-risk states that is essential to preventing outbreaks of ethnic violence. "Just as U.S. policy planners once spent enormous energy pinpointing likely

An understanding of different cultures allows world leaders to foster diplomacy as well as pinpoint areas where ethnic conflicts are likely to occur.

spots for Communist aggression, so too should they now be identifying future ethnic flashpoints," says David Callahan, project director for the Twentieth Century Fund, a research foundation that analyzes foreign policy. "Developing scenarios of how ethnic conflict in various countries might unfold would provide a crucial foundation for responding to fast-breaking crises."

Predicting ethnic violence

A knowledge of other cultures is key to understanding why and when ethnic conflict is likely to occur. Thus world leaders need to develop a deeper understanding of the basic religious and philosophical assumptions of other societies. This kind of knowledge is especially important as trade and communications networks bring cultures into closer contact with one another. Samuel Huntington has predicted that the "most important conflicts of the future will occur along the cultural fault lines separating civilizations from one another." This assertion is based on the fact that the people of different civilizations have very different conceptions of rights, responsibilities, equality, liberty, authority, religion, and the roles of men, women, and children in society. And because these different viewpoints are the result of deeply rooted traditions, they are not easily modified. Understanding cultural differences can facilitate diplomacy. In addition, when officials are armed with the knowledge of the history and culture of other groups, they may be able to recognize the warning signs of conflicts and prevent violence from erupting.

Warning signs

It is possible to forecast when and where ethnic violence is likely to erupt. There are warning signs which are known to signal the outbreak of violent conflict. When an empire is being constructed or maintained, as was the case with the Soviet Union, genocide is likely to occur as a method of land acquisition and as a way of subduing or intimidating a rebellious or stubborn population. If an ethnic group does not have a territory and lacks resources, ethnic violence may be directed at that group, as was the case with the Turkish Armenians in 1915. A subordinate ethnic community may also be left vulnerable to attack when a system of control collapses. The collapse of Yugoslavia led to Serb aggression against the Bosnian Muslims, and the breakup of the Ottoman Empire in Turkey led to the genocide of the Armenians by ethnic Turks.

When an ethnic group is privileged economically and socially but lacks military and political power, state genocide may occur. This was the case for Jews living in Europe at the time Adolf Hitler and the Nazi Party rose to power. Their genocide was facilitated because Hitler's totalitarian regime advanced an ideology that scapegoated the Jews. Ethnic violence is often imminent when a state holds an ideology that denounces or scapegoats one segment of the population. The state repression of ethnic minorities, or the tolerance of such repression, is another warning sign of ethnic violence. Ethnic repression includes not only the denial of political power sharing, but also acts such as desecrating religious sites and imposing a national language.

Exploiting ethnic antagonisms

Governments and political groups often foment ethnic strife for their own political gains. When this happens, it is a warning sign of ethnic violence. In 1993, Kenyan president Daniel arap Moi, determined to prove that multipartyism (the existence of more than one political party) would lead to ethnic conflicts, stirred up ethnic violence by fabricating and then publicizing tales of ethnic clashes between the Kikuyu people and Kenya's dominant ethnic group, the Kalenjin. Similarly, President Mobutu Sese Seko of Zaire instigated ethnic conflict that displaced and killed thousands. Mobutu's goal was to destabilize his political opposition and show that Zaire was ungovernable without him.

Such divide-and-conquer strategies are commonly used to fend off calls for democratization, with those in power claiming that democratization will only lead to ethnic strife. Political leaders take advantage of communal antagonisms and exploit them to help maintain their own power. Political parties based on ethnic groups are common in divided societies, and they are dangerous to political stability because of the possibility that one group will gain office and exclude other groups from resources and power. The rise of ethnically based political parties can be a warning sign of ethnic violence. In Rwanda, ethnically based political parties contributed to ethnic conflicts that later exploded in a genocide which the international community was criticized for failing to prevent.

Rwanda: a preventable horror?

Critics of U.S. foreign policy have charged that more could have been done to prevent the breakdown of order in Rwanda and assuage the genocidal campaign that broke out in April 1994. Alain Destexhe, secretary-general of Médecins Sans Frontières (Doctors Without Borders), stated that early action could have prevented genocide in Rwanda. According to Destexhe, "Deploying an intervention force early in a crisis can save not only lives but also money." In three and a half months during 1994, Rwandan genocide claimed 500,000 to 1 million lives, making it one of the greatest human rights disasters of our time. As many as 30,000 may have participated in the genocide orchestrated by the former Hutu regime, which planned to systematically eliminate Tutsis, as well as moderate Hutus who opposed plans for total Hutu domination.

There were warning signs that signaled the potential for violence between Hutu and Tutsi in Rwanda. Since the end of colonialism in 1959, when Hutu forces took over the country, the Tutsi have been persecuted. The Hutu ruling elite repressed the Tutsi, using discrimination and violence to retain power. After independence, an estimated 70 percent of the Tutsi population fled the country, and in the 1960s, more than fifteen thousand

Tutsis who remained in Rwanda were murdered. The Rwandan Patriotic Front (RPF), which invaded Rwanda in 1990 in an attempt to wrest the government from Hutu control, consisted mainly of Tutsi refugees and their descendants. Ironically, Rwanda had been the focus of international attention for several years prior to the outbreak of violence in 1994.

In 1992 the Organization of African Unity (OAU) established a military observer group to monitor a cease-fire and help end the two-year war between the Tutsi-led RPF and the Hutu-dominated Rwandan military. Under international pressure, negotiations between the Rwandan government and the RPF led to a peace agreement signed by both sides. The UN Security Council deployed a force of twenty-five hundred peacekeeping personnel, known as UNAMIR, to Rwanda. These troops were in place at the time the genocide began.

These young refugees are part of a group of nearly 500,000 Rwandans who fled to neighboring Zaire as RPF troops swept through the country.

Mass killings

The campaign of mass killing, which had been planned by the Hutu-dominated Rwandan army for months, began on April 6, 1994, immediately following the suspicious crash of an airplane carrying the presidents of both Rwanda and Burundi. The plane is believed to have been downed deliberately, although no one was ever convicted in connection with the incident. Within thirty minutes of the plane crash, roads out of Kigali were blocked and the killings began. Among the first victims was Prime Minister Agathe Uwilingiyimana, who was attempting to reach the UN compound when a mob of Hutu militiamen killed her. Belgian UNAMIR soldiers who tried to save her from the mob of soldiers were also murdered.

Prisoners await hearings by the Rwandan tribunal after being convicted of war crimes.

Consequently, Belgium, after evacuating its citizens from the country, withdrew its 420 soldiers from UNAMIR, leaving humanitarian groups unable to rally support to stop the genocide. "You can't overstate the impact on our policy process of the Belgians leaving," said Human Rights Watch director Holly Burkhalter. "People were saying, 'How can we get in, if it is so bad that the Belgians have to leave?'" During the first weeks of the crisis, the Security Council debated the fate of UNAMIR in Rwanda and ultimately voted to reduce the force to a 250-person skeleton crew. Burkhalter called the consequences of that vote for Rwanda "incalculable" in human terms.

The Canadian commander of the UNAMIR force has since stated that if he had received certain equipment, especially armored vehicles, he could have stemmed the genocide even without additional troops. But the reduction of UN forces and the international community's reluctance to respond to the crisis and failure to upgrade equipment then being used in Rwanda allowed the genocide to run unchecked, killing nearly half the Tutsi population. The holocaust ended in July with the victory of the RPF over the extremist Hutu regime. Rwanda's current multiparty interim government is headed by moderate Hutus but powered by the Tutsi-dominated Rwandan Patriotic

Front. There are reports that RPF soldiers have been taking revenge by killing returning Hutu refugees, making the world's worst refugee crisis even more desperate, as refugees flee once again out of fear of reprisal. An ad hoc Rwandan war crimes tribunal has been set up by the UN Security Council.

In the United States there was opposition by the Pentagon to an enhanced military presence in Rwanda, partly as a result of the American military experience in Somalia, where anarchy and civil war had made even humanitarian intervention difficult. Fearing that the United States would be called on to bail out a UN military force if things went badly, the Pentagon was reluctant to support a commitment to international engagement in Rwanda. Moreover, the Clinton administration's formal policy directive on the issue placed strong limits on the peacekeeping operations the United States would support.

Boutros Boutros-Ghali asked the Security Council to reconsider its decision to reduce the UNAMIR military presence in the face of the genocide, but to no avail. When the genocide was long over and Rwanda had instead a refugee crisis, U.S. troops were sent to participate in relief efforts among refugees in Rwanda and neighboring Zaire.

Lessons from Rwanda

One lesson from Rwanda has already been applied in the international community's enhanced concern for Burundi, which borders Rwanda and is similarly fraught with ethnic violence. The U.S. ambassador to Burundi has publicly warned the Burundian authorities, including military and political officials, against an outbreak of politically motivated ethnic violence. Better mechanisms for the provision of equipment in the face of crises have also been put in place.

The role foreign aid and development may have played in promoting ethnic violence has also been called into question in the aftermath of the Rwandan experience. Scholar Peter Uvin at Brown University's Watson Institute for International Studies says, "Those in the development community think there were no links between what they were doing and the genocide in Rwanda." Uvin, however, believes that "development aid, development discourse, and development agencies and experts are part of the same system as ethnic and communal attachments, oppression and discrimination, violence and genocide." Because development money provided jobs, land, and training for the elite or well connected, it served to increase tensions between groups as well as the disparity between rich and poor. According to Uvin, efforts to fund development in Rwanda without addressing the country's ethnic inequality, state-sponsored racism, and absence of justice actually contributed to these tensions. Thus development aid must be seen as an integral element of society in order to be applied constructively with the aim of avoiding conflict.

Conflict prevention

Preventive diplomacy tries to stop conflicts before they escalate to violence. Conflict prevention aims at the root causes of conflicts: poverty, excessive crowding, resource competition, environmental degradation, uncontrolled migration, economic instability, and the lack of viable political institutions. The U.S. Agency for International Development (USAID) believes that directing more money, time,

Ethiopian refugees have long been the victims of tribal conflict and drought. Poverty, overcrowding, and environmental degradation are just a few of the conditions that lead to ethnic violence.

and resources to these underlying causes will prevent future disasters. However, as the example of Rwanda shows, development funding does not solve ethnic concerns. Professor Stephen John Stedman has written, "one has to scrutinize the underlying assumption that foreign aid per se is conflict prevention. . . . There is the tacit belief that while underdevelopment induces conflict, development is somehow conflict-free. But this is not the case." Even if ethnic conflicts are unavoidable, early action can sometimes bring diplomatic settlements or at least contain violent outbursts.

According to *Foreign Policy* editor Charles William Maynes, preventive diplomacy can ensure that ethnic or religious tensions are addressed before they erupt into violence. For example, increased monitoring can make vital information about developments around the globe available to policymakers. The importance of early action to preventing conflicts was recognized by Secretary of State Warren Christopher, who noted that "the West has missed repeated opportunities to engage in early and effective ways that might have prevented the [Bosnian] conflict from deepening." Analysts believe that by identifying situations where ethnic groups are being persecuted, and then intervening on behalf of that group's rights, conflict can be prevented.

Protecting ethnic minorities

An underlying cause of ethnic conflict is a lack of respect for minority rights. The United Nations has begun to pay more attention to minority rights and to encourage the development of civil states where all citizens enjoy equal rights. "Moral approval must go to the civil state, which seeks to provide a decent life for all of its citizens," according to *Foreign Policy*, "rather than to the ethnic state, which provides a home for a dominant nationality." A growing number of world leaders and opinion shapers have begun to state outright that massive human rights violations as well as domestic policies such as racial discrimination and genocide "should not be tolerated by the community of civilized nations." The international community can create a climate that is inhospitable to the mistreatment of minorities. States that violate human rights can be sanctioned by denying them access to international markets or financial institutions and suspending their membership in international organizations. If early action is taken to protest the poor treatment of minorities within a state, escalation of ethnic conflict may be avoided by forcing state leaders to peacefully address ethnic concerns before they become explosive.

Sometimes, when states create and exploit ethnic conflict, the international community can stop the cycle by coercing the countries at fault through cuts in foreign aid and crippling economic sanctions. Such actions, however, can create severe hardships for the civilian populations of target countries. Two UN agencies, the International Monetary Fund and the International Bank for Reconstruction and Development (World Bank), also can revoke loans to governments that repress ethnic minorities. "Realistically, world opinion alone cannot prevent a large state from mistreating its minorities if it is determined to do so," says Charles William Maynes. "But criticism, ostracism, and sanctions can affect decision making. And most states are not in a position to defy the international community totally."

Economic sanctions send a message that countries will have to pay a price for their abuse through restricted access to international aid. As David Callahan, project director at the Twentieth Century Fund, suggests, governments with the best human rights records could be placed at the top of the list of recipients for economic aid and debt relief, while nations with the worst reputations could be denied aid altogether. Some countries, however, fear that Western-dominated development agencies and international organizations may not take into account the interests of smaller states.

Fear of Western domination

The West dominates international political and security institutions, yet decisions made by these institutions are said to reflect the interests of the "world community." As a result, some developing member nations fear that the more powerful countries hold unfair advantages. During the UN peacekeeping operation in Somalia, for example, a Pakistani peacekeeper explained, "The U.S. is quick to stir up trouble with air strikes, but it is my men and other third world soldiers who always draw the tough assignments on the ground." According to the editor of *Foreign Policy*:

> Many developing countries are reluctant to see the Security Council, dominated by five permanent members [China, France, Russia, the United Kingdom, and the United States], of which [all but China] are former colonial powers, as the chief enforcement instrument of intervention to maintain international peace and security and to protect minority rights.

The use of regional organizations

One way in which nations have attempted to allay this fear is by strengthening regional organizations that involve local peoples in settling disputes. The West African states have intervened in the Liberian civil war. In Latin America, the Contadora Group, composed of Latin American states, was able to positively influence warring factions within the region. Regional groups may become partisan, however, as has been the case with the Arab League, which harshly criticized Israel's human rights violations while ignoring abuses in the Arab world. This partisanship stems from the conflict between Arabs and Jews, who both claim ownership rights to some of the same land in the Middle East. Using regional organizations to resolve existing conflicts can be problematic if the members of the groups are too close to the conflict themselves to deal with it effectively. This was also the case in the 1970s when the Organization of African Unity turned a blind eye while Ugandan dictator Idi Amin committed gross human rights violations against ethnic groups in Uganda who did not support his regime. On the premise that regional groups have the power to influence surrounding states, U.S. policy analysts have decided that concentrating on key regional states may be an effective way of dealing with ethnic conflicts and global security.

Identifying pivotal states

In the search for new principles on which to base U.S. foreign policy, analysts suggest that the United States must develop more than one strategy to confront many of today's global challenges and conflicts. America's national interest requires stability in key areas of the developing world. There are many pivotal states—developing countries whose futures will influence their surrounding regions—that have the power to affect regional and international stability. Their collapse could lead to more conflicts, refugee crises, and a disruption in the region's trade patterns. Pivotal states are those with large populations, critical geographical locations, and economic potential. Ensuring the stability of these states may make it possible to maintain security within an entire region. Mexico, Brazil, Algeria, Egypt, South Africa, Turkey, India, Pakistan, and Indonesia are currently considered by scholars to be pivotal states.

South Africa, for example, is a pivotal state for the region of sub-Saharan Africa. It has successfully made the transition from apartheid (a government policy of racial discrimination) to a reconciliation government with a healthy respect for ethnic differences. With a sound currency, strong infrastructure (system of internal organization), and vast natural resources, South Africa has the potential to stimulate growth throughout Africa. However, ethnic conflict and political instability still plague South Africa. Internal threats could reverse the progress that has been made. "If [South Africa] prospers, it can show other ethnically tortured regions a path to stability through democratization, reconciliation, and steadily increasing living standards," write three Yale historians. "Alternatively, if it fails to handle its many challenges, it will suck its neighbors into a whirlpool of self-defeating conflict."

With its strategic location between Europe and Asia, bridging the worlds of Islam and Christianity, Turkey is also a pivotal state with the power to influence many countries. Turkey has been an example of secularism and tolerance, but its democratic institutions are threatened by overpopulation, the challenge of ethnic minorities, and a rise in Islamic fundamentalism. Likewise, India and Pakistan both face extreme population pressures, as workers there already outnumber job opportunities. In India, militant Hindus and Muslims challenge democratic traditions, and Islam fuels nationalist sentiment in Pakistan. The two countries have warred over neighboring Kashmir, and each continues to arm itself against the other. A conflict between the two could escalate to involve the wider region, including Kashmir and Afghanistan, and also entails the threat of nuclear warfare. Therefore, the United States is committed to maintaining peace and stability in these parts of Asia.

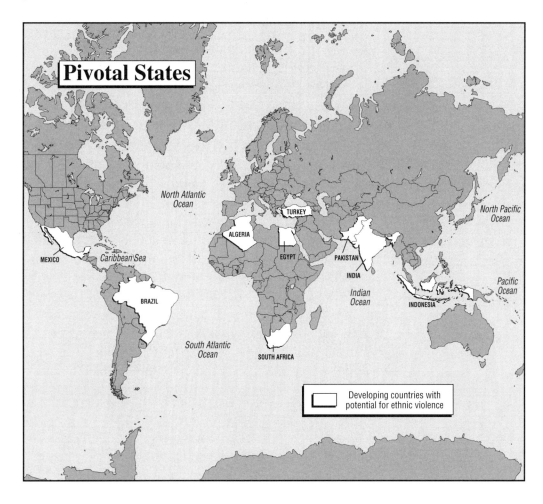

Allocating resources selectively

By focusing on pivotal states, those that are most important to U.S. national interests, resources can be allocated with greater effectiveness. Perhaps more can be accomplished by funneling relatively large amounts of economic aid to pivotal states than by dispersing funds in smaller amounts to a greater number of countries. This policy attempts to deal with problems selectively by responding to them according to their ability to affect a region. Focusing on key states may also restore the American public's confidence in foreign aid. According to scholars Robert S. Chase, Emily B. Hill, and Paul Kennedy:

> American policymakers, themselves less and less willing to contemplate foreign obligations, are acutely aware that the public is extremely cautious about and even hostile toward overseas engagements. While the American public may not reject all such commitments, it does resist intervention in areas that appear peripheral to U.S. interests.

If policymakers want the support of the American public, then, it may be essential to intervene in foreign states selectively and strategically. Helping to maintain peace and prosperity in pivotal states may go a long way to prevent ethnic violence, as well as contain it from spreading to other regions.

Although ethnic conflict may be inevitable in the modern world, prevention techniques such as understanding other cultures, recognizing the warning signs of ethnic violence, developing a plan of action that aims to remedy the underlying causes of conflict, and focusing on key states can, in some cases, bring about diplomatic settlements, or at least help to contain violent outbursts. When its goal is to prevent disaster rather than react to it, policy can work to stop the spread of chaos and civil unrest which threatens the lives and security of so many around the planet.

Glossary

autonomy: Self-government; in modern times, understood to be a right.

cold war: Term used to describe the post–World War II competition for influence between the United States and the USSR that was supported by military action but did not result in the termination of diplomatic ties.

communism: A political philosophy proposing the elimination of private property; the official doctrine of the former Soviet Union, in which a totalitarian government controlled the means of production.

containment: The policy or process of preventing the expansion of a hostile power or ideology.

ethnicity: A social grouping comprising individuals who share aspects of a common culture, including some combination of the following traits: race, appearance, language, religion, and common origin.

ethnocide: The destruction of an ethnic group, also known as ethnic cleansing. Ethnocide can be accomplished through killing or by destroying a group's culture and assimilating them so that they cease to exist as a unique group.

ethno-nationalism: A particular form of nationalism that is based on ethnic, rather than civic, identity.

fundamentalism: A movement or attitude that stresses strict and literal adherence to a set of basic principles, often religious.

human rights: The ideas, recognized by the United Nations, that all people, because they are human, have certain basic rights, and that these rights apply to all humans equally.

indigenous: That which originates in and is native to a particular region or environment.

nationalism: A system of ideas and values shared by a community of individuals who have a common language, character, and culture, and who are all subordinate to a state power that reflects their common interests.

North Atlantic Treaty Organization (NATO): An organization developed to implement the North Atlantic Treaty of 1949, which sought to establish a counterweight for the Soviet military presence in Europe after WWII. Today NATO continues as a collective defense agreement between the Western powers, and it operates as an organization devoted to maintaining international stability in Europe.

Sinn Féin (pronounced Shin Fane): An Irish political and cultural society founded around 1905 to promote political and economic independence from England, the unification of Ireland, and a renewal of Irish culture. Today Sinn Féin constitutes the political arm of the Irish Republican Army (IRA).

sovereignty: Freedom from external control, i.e., an autonomous state.

United Nations (UN): An international organization founded at the end of WWII whose primary purpose is to maintain international peace and security. Today the UN consists of 185 member states.

xenophobia: Fear and hatred of strangers and foreigners.

Organizations
to Contact

American Anti-Slavery Group (AASG)
PO Box 441612
W. Somerville, MA 02144
(617) 278-4342

AASG works to publicize the plight of child and adult slaves in Africa and Asia in order to make Americans aware of the persistence of slavery in the world. The group publishes a newsletter and hosts conferences.

Amnesty International USA (AIUSA)
322 Eighth Ave.
New York, NY 10001
(212) 807-8400

AIUSA works impartially for the release of men, women, and children detained anywhere in the world for their conscientiously held beliefs, color, ethnic origin, sex, religion, or language, provided they have neither used nor advocated violence. Publications include a newsletter and an annual report.

Brookings Institution
1775 Massachusetts Ave. NW
Washington, DC 20036-2188
(202) 797-6000

Brookings is an independent organization devoted to nonpartisan research, education, and publication in the fields of economics, government, and foreign policy; it publishes a quarterly newsletter and an annual report.

Center for War/Peace Studies
218 E. Eighteenth St.
New York, NY 10003
(212) 475-1077

The center conducts studies on various global problems, including ethnic conflicts. It advocates arms control and disarmament, seeks a Middle East peace settlement, and works to move the world beyond violent conflict and toward international cooperation under law. The center publishes the quarterly newsletter *Global Report: Progress Toward a World of Peace and Justice.*

Council on Foreign Relations
58 E. Sixty-eighth St.
New York, NY 10021
(212) 734-0400

The council specializes in knowledge of foreign affairs and studies the international aspects of American political and economic policies and problems. Its journal *Foreign Affairs*, published five times a year, includes analyses of current ethnic conflicts around the world.

Doctors Without Borders (Médecins Sans Frontières)
11 E. Twenty-sixth St., #1904
New York, NY 10010
(212) 679-6800

A multinational organization of medical professionals that provides assistance to victims of war and natural disasters. Doctors Without Borders publishes a free newsletter, *Alert*, three times a year, which contains articles on the areas where Doctors Without Borders is active. An annual book, which examines five countries in crisis and the humanitarian response, is also published.

Human Rights Watch (HRW)
485 Fifth Ave.
New York, NY 10017-6104
(212) 972-8400

HRW comprises groups and individuals who promote and monitor human rights worldwide. It evaluates the human rights practices of governments according to standards set by international laws and agreements. HRW serves as an umbrella organization for affiliated regional groups such as Asia Watch and Middle East Watch. Each group publishes periodic newsletters and reports.

Institute for the Study of Genocide (ISG)
John Jay College of Criminal Justice
899 Tenth Ave., Room 623
New York, NY 10019
(212) 582-2537

An association of professors, scholars, and individuals united to study the causes, prevention, and consequences of genocide and to sponsor predictive research on the causes of genocide. ISG also monitors contemporary reports of human rights violations and considers strategies to impede genocide as well as to assist potential victims. Publishes *ISG Newsletter* semiannually.

Project on Ethnic Relations
One Palmer Square, Suite 435
Princeton, NJ 08542
(609) 683-5666

The project is a research organization that studies ethnic relations in the new European democracies. It seeks the peaceful resolution of ethnic conflicts there, in part by encouraging mediation and negotiation. Publications include conference reports and the quarterly *Project on Ethnic Relations Bulletin.*

The Twentieth Century Fund (TCF)
41 E. Seventieth St.
New York, NY 10021
(212) 535-4441

The fund is a research foundation that sponsors and supervises timely analyses of economic policy, foreign affairs, politics and governance, and media issues. TCF publishes an annual report.

Suggestions for Further Reading

Susan Banfield, *Ethnic Conflicts in Schools*. Springfield, NJ: Enslow, 1995. An overview of why conflicts occur among students and how some have attempted to resolve them.

Charles P. Cozic, ed., *Nationalism and Ethnic Conflict*. San Diego: Greenhaven Press, 1994. This book contains essays on the positive and negative aspects of nationalism, as well as opposing viewpoints on why ethnic violence is or is not justified.

Donald Horowitz, *Ethnic Groups in Conflict*. Berkeley: University of California Press, 1985. Using case studies from around the globe, this book analyzes ethnic conflict through a series of essays devoted to different regional conflicts.

Caroline Meyer, *Voices of Northern Ireland: Growing Up in a Troubled Land*. San Diego: Harcourt Brace Jovanovich, 1987. Based on the American author's travels in Northern Ireland, this book portrays what daily life is like for those who live in conflict-ridden Northern Ireland.

Works Consulted

Books

Rabian Ali and Lawrence Lifschultz, eds., *Why Bosnia: Writings on the Balkan War.* Stony Creek, CT: The Pamphleteer's Press, 1993. A collection of essays on the conflict that engulfed Bosnia-Herzegovina following the breakup of Yugoslavia in 1991.

Miron Dolot, *Execution by Hunger: The Hidden Holocaust.* New York: W.W. Norton, 1985. A survivor of the Ukrainian famines tells his story of the collectivization policies of the USSR.

Harold Isaacs, *Power and Identity: Tribalism in World Politics.* New York: Foreign Policy Association, 1979. A pamphlet in the SUNY foreign policy series that examines the role of foreign policy in provoking and stemming ethnic conflict.

Michael T. Klare, ed., *World Security.* New York: St. Martin's Press, 1994. Collection of essays devoted to issues of world security, ethnic conflict, and disarmament.

Walter Laqueur, *Europe in Our Time.* New York: Viking, 1992. Western, Central, and Eastern European history since World War II resource book.

René Lemarchand, *Burundi: Ethnocide as Discourse and Practice.* Cambridge, England: Cambridge University Press, 1994. This book explores the history of ethnic conflict between the Hutu and Tutsi in Burundi, including the events leading to recent outbreaks of violence in Burundi.

David McKittrick, *Endgame: The Search for Peace in Northern Ireland*. Belfast: The Blackstaff Press, 1994. A collection of reports and commentary on recent events in Northern Ireland.

Joseph V. Montville, ed., *Conflict and Peacemaking in Multiethnic Societies*. Lexington, MA: Lexington Books, 1990. A series of essays on the nature of the nation-state, theories of conflict management and power sharing, and the role of politics in ethnic conflicts, including case studies of Northern Ireland, Sri Lanka, and North and sub-Saharan Africa.

Manning P. Nash, *Unfinished Agenda: The Dynamics of Modernization in Developing Countries*. Chicago: University of Chicago Press, 1984. Discusses issues of modernization and colonialism, giving an account of social changes since the end of empires and the birth of new nations in old societies.

Binaifer Nowrojee, *Divide and Rule: State-Sponsored Ethnic Violence in Kenya*. New York: Human Rights Watch, 1993. Discusses the role that government-fomented ethnic clashes played in the attempt to prevent the advent of multipartyism in Kenya.

William Petersen, ed., *The Background to Ethnic Conflict*. Leiden, Netherlands: E. J. Brill, 1979. Collection of essays providing a global perspective on the causes and histories of ethnic conflicts.

Richard Polenberg, *One Nation Divisible: Class, Race, and Ethnicity in the U.S. Since 1938*. New York: Penguin, 1980. Social history of class, race, and ethnic conflicts and divisions in American history since the 1930s.

Ngugi Wa Thiong'o, *Moving the Centre: The Struggle for Cultural Freedoms*. Nairobi: English Press, 1993. Discusses the need to free world cultures from Western domination as well as the restrictions of nationalism, class, race, and gender.

J. Milton Yinger, *Ethnicity: Source of Strength? Source of Conflict?* New York: State University of New York Press, 1994. This book presents opposing viewpoints on ethnicity and examines how it can be both a uniting and divisive force.

Periodicals

Holly Burkhalter, "A Preventable Horror?" *Africa Report*, November/December 1994, p. 18.

David Callahan, "Confronting Ethnic Conflict," *Foreign Service Journal*, October 1994, p. 33.

Robert S. Chase, Emily B. Hill, and Paul Kennedy, "Pivotal States and U.S. Strategy," *Foreign Affairs*, January/February 1996, p. 35.

Roger Cohen, "Karadzic's Bosnian War: Myth Becomes Madness," *New York Times*, June 4, 1995, p. 14:1.

John Colarusso, "Chechnya: The War Without Winners," *Current History*, October 1995, pp. 329, 334.

Alan Cooperman, "A Trail of Tears from Grozy to Nowhere," *U.S. News & World Report*, February 27, 1995, pp. 60–61.

Brian Eads, "Slavery's Shameful Return to Africa," *Reader's Digest*, March 1996, p. 80.

Economist, "Sudan's Old Secessionists Try a New Strategy," December 9, 1995, p. 43.

Economist, "Unwanted, Uncounted," June 24, 1995, p. 44.

Dorinda Elliot and Steve Levine, "An Ethnic Nightmare in the Caucasus," *Newsweek*, December 7, 1992, p. 34.

Vaclav Havel, "The New Measure of Man," *New York Times*, July 8, 1994, p. A27.

Barry Hillenbrand, "Afterlife of Violence," *Time*, June 12, 1995, p. 58.

Lindsey Hillsum, "Rwanda: Settling Scores," *Africa Report*, May/June 1994, pp. 13–17.

Geoffrey Howe, "Sovereignty, Democracy, and Human Rights," *Political Quarterly*, July–September 1995, p. 129.

Samuel P. Huntington, "The Clash of Civilizations?" *Foreign Affairs*, Summer 1993, p. 27.

Jeremiah Kamau, "Rwanda's Trail of Tears," *U.S. News & World Report*, May 16, 1994, pp. 10–11.

Mark N. Katz, "Nationalism and the Legacy of Empire," *Current History*, October 1994, pp. 327–31.

Edmund J. Keller, "The Ethnogenesis of the Oromo Nation and Its Political Implications for Ethiopia," *Journal of Modern African Studies*, vol. 33, no. 4, 1995, pp. 621–25.

Robin Knight, "The Hunt for the Killers of Bosnia," *U.S. News & World Report*, April 10, 1995, p. 53.

Colum Lynch, "Battle over International Court," *Boston Globe*, April 7, 1996, p. 15.

Edward D. Mansfield and Jack Snyder, "Democratization and War," *Foreign Affairs,* May/June 1995, p. 79.

Charles William Maynes, "Containing Ethnic Conflict," *Foreign Policy*, Summer 1993, p. 19.

John McGarry and Brendan O'Leary, "The Political Regulation of National and Ethnic Conflict," *Parliamentary Affairs,* January 1994, pp. 94–115.

Marguerite Michaels, "Somalia: Peacemaking War," *Time*, July 26, 1993, p. 48.

Peter Moszynski, "Edge of the Abyss," *New Statesman and Society*, July 14, 1995, pp. 22–23.

Andrew Phillips, "The Gates Slam Shut," *Maclean's*, June 14, 1993, p. 19.

James M. Prince, "A Kurdish State in Iraq?" *Current History*, January 1993, pp. 17–22.

Richard Schultz, "State Disintegration and Ethnic Conflict," *Annals of the American Academy of Political and Social Science*, September 1995, p. 79.

Benjamin Schwarz, "The Diversity Myth: America's Leading Export," *Atlantic*, May 1995, p. 58.

John Stephen Stedman, "Alchemy for a New World Order," *Foreign Affairs*, May/June 1995, pp. 14–20.

U.S. Dept. of State Dispatch, "Implementing the Dayton Agreements: New Partnerships," vol. 7, no. 7, February 12, 1996, pp. 33–38.

U.S. News & World Report, "American Versus Aidid," October 25, 1993, pp. 34–35.

Peter Uvin, "Challenging Current Development Practice," *Brown Journal on Third World Affairs*, Spring 1995, pp. 3–7.

Albert Wohlstetter and Gregory S. Jones, "Alternatives to Negotiating Genocide," *Wall Street Journal*, May 3, 1995, p. A24.

Victor Zaslavsky, "Nationalism and Democratic Transition," *Daedalus*, Spring 1992, pp. 107, 112.

Index

About the Author

Mary Hull has a B.A. in history from Brown University. She is a freelance writer and lives in Boston, where she writes for educational publishers and businesses. In recent years, Ms. Hull has lived in Kenya, studying the oral traditions of the Luo.

Picture Credits

Cover photo: © Christopher Morris/Time/Black Star
AFP/Bettmann, 59
AFP/Corbis-Bettmann, 16, 36
Archive Photos/Camera Press, 42
Archive Photos/Reuters, 63
Archive Photos/Reuters/Arthur Tsang, 18
Archive Photos/Reuters/Corinne Dufka, 46, 88
Archive Photos/Reuters/Darren Whiteside, 68
Archive Photos/Reuters/Fatih Saribas, 77
Archive Photos/Reuters/Peter Jones, 56
Archive Photos/Reuters/Sunil Malhatra, 53
Archive Photos/Reuters/Volodia Smalikov, 15
© Alexandra Avakian/Woodfin Camp & Associates, Inc., 60
© 1992 Donna Binder/Impact Visuals, 30
© Enrico Dagnino/Cosmos/Woodfin Camp & Associates, Inc., 27, 49
FAO photo by F. Botts, 84
© 1995 Sue Hostetler/Impact Visuals, 38
© Barry Iverson/Woodfin Camp & Associates, Inc., 24
© Catherine Karnow/Woodfin Camp & Associates, Inc., 10
Library of Congress, 34, 62
National Archives, 35
Photo by B. Press courtesy of UNHCR, 90 (neg. #22047)
Photos by A. Hollmann courtesy of UNHCR, 13 (neg. #22029), 79 (neg. #21016)
Reuters/Corbis-Bettmann, 31, 43, 70, 74, 87
© 1992 Lester Sloan/Woodfin Camp & Associates, Inc., 22
© Ted Soqui/Impact Visuals, 20
UN photo 161941/Milton Grant, 72
UPI/Corbis-Bettmann, 29
WHO photo by Wolmuth, 7